Ambrosiana at Harvard:

New Sources of Milanese Chant

Edited by

Thomas Forrest Kelly

and Matthew Mugmon

Houghton Library of the Harvard College Library

Cambridge, Massachusetts

2010

Distributed by Harvard University Press

Houghton Library Studies

Series Editor: William P. Stoneman

Houghton Library Studies provides a forum for
the scholarly analysis of the wide-ranging materials in
the collections of Houghton Library, the primary
repository for rare books and manuscripts
at Harvard University.

*This volume has been published with income from
the George L. Lincoln, Class of 1895, Publication Fund.*

Library of Congress Cataloging-in-Publication Data

Ambrosiana at Harvard: new sources of Milanese chant / edited by Thomas Forrest Kelly and Matthew Mugmon.
    p.   cm. — (Houghton library studies)
    Includes bibliographical references.
    ISBN 978-0-9818858-0-3 (alk. paper)
  1. Ambrosian chants—History and criticism. I. Kelly, Thomas Forrest. II. Mugmon, Matthew.
    ML3070.A53 2010
    782.32'220094521—dc22

2010010749

Contents

Illustrations

The contributors to this volume kindly acknowledge the following archives and libraries for making their collections accessible and for granting permission to reproduce images: Benevento, Biblioteca Capitolare (5.3, 5.4, 5.5, 5.11); Cambridge, Mass., Houghton Library (figs. 1.2, 1.4, 1.6, 1.8, 2.1, 2.2, 2.3, 3.3, 3.4, 3.6, 3.9, 3.10, 3.11, 3.12, 3.13, 3.17, 3.20, 5.4, 5.10, 5.12, 5.13, 7.1, 8.1); Gallarate, Archivio di Santa Maria Assunta (1.3, 1.4, 1.5); London, British Library (3.1, 3.5, 3.7, 3.8, 3.14, 3.15, 3.16, 3.20, 3.21, 5.11); Mariano Comense, Archivio Santo Stefano (4.1, 4.2, 4.6); Milan, Biblioteca Ambrosiana, Copyright Biblioteca Ambrosiana—Auth No. 08/0393 (2.1, 2.2, 2.3); Milan, Biblioteca Capitolare (3.18, 3.19, 3.20); Milan, Pontifical Ambrosian Institute of Sacred Music, Photo Library (3.2); Montecassino, Archivio della Badia (5.1, 5.2); Novara, Archivio Storico Diocesano (1.7); Paris, Bibliothèque nationale de France (6.1); Rome, Biblioteca Vallicelliana, by permission of the Ministero per i Beni e le Attività Culturali; further reproduction or duplication by any means is prohibited (5.6, 5.8, 5.9, 5.10, 5.11, 5.13); Vatican City, Biblioteca Apostolica Vaticana (3.2, 5.12). Contributors have made every effort to provide detailed information on images, including institutional call numbers and real measurements of the material shown, with height given first, in centimeters. In some cases, however, the circumstances in which some images were captured did not allow complete data to be obtained.

Tables

Acknowledgments

THIS VOLUME OWES THE QUALITY OF ITS CONTENTS to its parentage in the Houghton Library and its good looks to its family resemblance to the Houghton Library Studies series. We are grateful to William Stoneman, Florence Fearrington Librarian of the Houghton Library, for his support throughout the development of this project—from the acquisition of manuscripts through the planning and support of a conference to the preparation and publication of this volume.

The staff of the Houghton Library have been unfailingly helpful and collaborative. Dennis Marnon, Administrative Officer of the Library, has patiently shepherded this wayward volume into its fold; Monique Duhaime wisely and inventively assisted in the coordination of the 2007 exhibition and conference.

The conference "Ambrosiana at Harvard," whose proceedings are described in the introduction, was made possible with the support of the Houghton Library, the Harvard Committee on Medieval Studies, the Harvard Department of Music, the Dean for the Humanities, the Harvard Humanities Center, the Provostial Fund for Arts and Humanities, and the Harvard Divinity School. It was a moment of interdisciplinary collaboration, as demonstrated by the wide-ranging nature of its supporters.

An exhibition mounted in connection with the exhibition was curated by Anna Zayaruznaya, who prepared a checklist of relevant Harvard material and assisted tirelessly in many details of the conference itself.

We thank Fredric and Susan Finkelstein for the loan to the exhibition of their handsome Ambrosian leaf. We are grateful to St. Paul's Church, Cambridge, and its mellifluous pastor, the Reverend Robert Congdon, for their hospitality and collaboration in the performance of vespers in Ambrosian chant. We were honored by the presence of Ferdinando Massetti, Luca Corbetta, and Alessandro Mazzini, members of the Cappella Musicale di Sant'Ambrogio, Milan, and their director, Maestro Giovanni Scomparin, for their musical embellishment of the scholarly proceedings.

We are grateful to those who assisted in many ways the research involved in this volume. Drew Massey, a member of the 2003 research seminar, is the developer of Inventoriana, an online collaborative inventorying tool that allowed students to formulate preliminary inventories of the Houghton manuscripts.

In the course of research and of a group research trip, a number of institutions have been particularly helpful. In particular we would like to acknowledge

Monsignor Marco Navoni of the Biblioteca Ambrosiana; dottor Fausto Ruggieri of the Biblioteca del Capitolo del Duomo; the Preside of the Pontificio Istituto Ambrosiano di Musica Sacra, Monsignor GianLuigi Rusconi, and the Institute's Secretary General, Giordano Monzio Compagnoni.

The preparation of this volume owes its largest debt to its contributors, who have been friends, teachers, and students of the editors and sometimes of one another. Our deep thanks go to each of them. Professor Joseph Dyer read a preliminary version of this volume, and with deep erudition and incomparable delicacy made suggestions that have improved it considerably. Dr. Thomas Kozachek, an expert in matters musical, liturgical, stylistic, and typographical, has enhanced the accuracy and appearance of this book enormously.

INTRODUCTION

Thomas Forrest Kelly

This volume brings together a group of studies of the music of the Ambrosian liturgy. Sung in and around medieval Milan, the Ambrosian chant is practiced to this day. Owing perhaps to the protection of the great doctor of the church and bishop of Milan, Ambrosian chant was not suppressed, like so many other dialects of liturgical music, by the Carolingian urge to impose the universal Roman liturgy and the chant now known as Gregorian. To the extent that these older practices can be recovered and studied, we can have a clearer picture of the early medieval cultural landscape, and a better sense of the aesthetic variety of medieval music.

William Stoneman, Florence Fearrington Librarian of the Houghton Library, was present along with Jeffrey Hamburger and Thomas Kelly, at a magical Saturday morning exploratory session in which the group of three sought to identify manuscripts in the library's holdings that would be suitable material for study in a jointly taught graduate seminar on illuminated manuscripts that included liturgical music. It was on that occasion that we opened Houghton Library MS Typ 299 and realized that it was a book of Ambrosian chant. In itself this was an interesting discovery, for sources of Ambrosian chant are rare outside the area of Milan, and rare indeed in North America. The book did serve as material for an unpublished preliminary investigation by Matthias Röder in 2003.

When two manuscripts of Ambrosian chant became available in 2004, it seemed something of a miracle that they could become part of the collection of the Houghton Library. It is owing to the foresight of William Stoneman—as well as that of the supporters of the Houghton Library—that these manuscripts of Ambrosian chant could be added to Harvard's collections as MS Lat 388 and MS Lat 389. The "new" manuscripts had been previously noted as being in a private collection, but this was only determined in the course of research after the manuscripts reached Harvard. The Houghton Library generously caused all three of the manuscripts to be digitized and made available online through the Harvard University Library's Page Delivery Service, where they may be consulted through the Harvard College Library's online catalog.

A pair of graduate seminars in musicology, in 2005 and 2006, allowed a group of researchers to study and inventory the manuscripts and to begin an appreciation of their place in the history of one of the important dialects of Western liturgical chant. A group of researchers from both seminars was able, through the generosity of the Morrill Fund of the Harvard Music Department, to travel to Milan in 2007 to examine relevant manuscripts in the Biblioteca del Capitolo del Duomo, the Biblioteca Ambrosiana, the Archivio di Santa Maria Assunta in Gallarate, and the Archivio Storico Diocesano of Novara and to consult the resources of the Pontifical Ambrosian Institute of Sacred Music.

The growing sense of the significance of the Harvard manuscripts, especially as a group, and of the considerable work that had already been undertaken, led the Houghton Library to sponsor a conference in October 2007, at which the papers in this volume were delivered in an earlier form.

The Houghton Library arranged an exhibition of manuscripts in connection with the conference, presenting the Houghton Ambrosiana and related documents; the exhibition was curated by Anna Zayaruznaya.

The conference was embellished with the presence of members of the Cappella Musicale della Basilica di Sant'Ambrogio, with their director, Maestro Giovanni Scomparin. These singers, along with a group from Harvard, performed Vespers of Saint Luke the Evangelist in Ambrosian chant, celebrated by the Reverend Robert J. Congdon, as the opening event of the conference; and the singers of Sant'Ambrogio enriched the conference with their performances of musical selections to open each day's proceedings.

The present volume considers the Houghton manuscripts of Ambrosian chant as physical objects, in their urban and historical contexts, and in the musical and ecclesiastical context of Milan, of Italy, and of medieval Europe. It seeks to provide an example of interdisciplinary collaboration and to show just how much can be learned from individual objects subjected to sustained scholarly scrutiny.

The volume begins with three studies having a relatively close focus on the manuscripts at the Houghton Library, and it continues with widening horizons to consider broader aspects of Ambrosian liturgy and music.

Mattias Röder and Jessica Berenbeim, in their study of Houghton Library MS Typ 299, are able to show that it forms part of a larger manuscript, whose other sections are at the library of Santa Maria Assunta in Gallarate. Together the manuscripts form a summer portion of the liturgy; a related manuscript, a winter portion, is now in the Archivio Storico Diocesano of Novara. The authors clarify the identity of the scribes of these manuscripts. Particularly interesting about this group is the extent to which they correspond to the Benedictine liturgy as performed in the Roman rite; the adaptation of Ambrosian music to monastic practice is a rarity, found, apparently, only in this group of manuscripts.

In his study of Houghton Library MS Lat 389, Matthew Mugmon shows that it is the "sibling" of a manuscript in the Biblioteca Ambrosiana at Milan (MS M 99 sup.). A survey of physical characteristics, layout, paleography, and decoration demonstrates the remarkable likeness of the two manuscripts, made in the late thirteenth or early fourteenth century. They are not separated parts of the same volume, nor are they winter and summer portions of the same set, but they appear to have been made by the same scribe. Differences in spelling, rubrical text, and liturgical arrangement are slight. The author suggests that the two books were made for the same church, yet to be identified.

MS Lat 388 is one of the oldest surviving manuscripts of Ambrosian chant, dating perhaps from the late twelfth century. It provides important evidence about a notational peculiarity of Ambrosian manuscripts, a horizontal green line that indicates the presence of B-flat. Such lines have often been thought to be later additions to manuscripts originally made without them. In an impressive array of paleographical and codicological findings, Anna Zayaruznaya analyses and describes the copying and revision of four Ambrosian antiphoners. The "green lines" in the title are the starting point for an investigation with a number of significant observations and conclusions.

The surprising durability of the Ambrosian chant is demonstrated by Angelo Rusconi, who reports on a number of hitherto unknown sources of Ambrosian chant ranging from the sixteenth to the nineteenth century. The extraordinary richness of the sources of the Renaissance and modern traditions is likely to be a revelation to most scholars. They describe the living tradition of Ambrosian chant—a tradition that also illustrates change in musical style and repertory.

The earliest surviving manuscripts of Ambrosian chant, like MS Lat 388, date from the twelfth century, but I demonstrate that the repertory existed in written form at least as far back as the eleventh. The evidence is indirect, for scribes in southern Italy copied excerpts from the Ambrosian repertory at that time, using notational peculiarities otherwise unknown in the south, which arose as a result of copying from now-lost Ambrosian sources.

Two eminent scholars reflect here on aspects of the liturgy of the Ambrosian rite, drawing on information in the Houghton manuscripts and elsewhere. Michel Huglo (whose catalog of Ambrosian sources, *Fonti e paleografia de canto ambrosiano*, was published more than fifty years ago, in 1956) considers antiphonal psalmody of the office. His essay is very wide ranging—an impressive introduction witnessing his knowledge of the sources leads to a treatment of the special Ambrosian relationship between the final and the reciting tone of the following psalmody.

Terence Bailey's contribution is a detailed study of the Milanese acceptance and liturgical implementation of the feast of Christmas, particularly with respect to the number of masses celebrated. The feast at Milan goes back at least to the time of Saint Ambrose, and Bailey's description of the gradual addition of a second and a third mass makes for fascinating reading.

Two contributions consider constituent genres of Ambrosian chant from very different analytical perspectives. John McKay's study is a preliminary analysis of the verses of the Ambrosian responsories of the office. In other kinds of chant (Old Roman and Gregorian) these are sung to standard formulas, but the presence of such formulas is far from clear in the Ambrosian repertory. Although some 40 percent of verse melodies appear to be independent compositions, McKay is able to demonstrate an underlying formulaic structure for most of the rest. The formulaic verses are tripartite, like the invitatory of the office as sung in the Roman rite. McKay's methods and classification system are of an admirable clarity and usefulness.

A very different set of analytical tools is applied to the *melodiae secundae* of the chant *Et lilia convalium* by Sasha Siem. Her quantitative analysis illustrates the progress from stepwise to ever-larger non-stepwise intervals. The author provides a meticulous examination and interpretation of every melodic gesture; these analyses will challenge scholars of the chant to scrutinize more closely every melody they study.

The varying scholarly methods employed in these papers and the expanding horizon they present—beginning with the Harvard manuscripts and placing them in paleographical, historical, and artistic contexts—provide, we hope, a panorama of an important cultural patrimony and of the ways in which medieval repertories can profitably be studied.

Milanese Chant in the Monastery?

Notes on a Reunited Ambrosian Manuscript

Jessica Berenbeim and Matthias Röder

WHEN PHILIP HOFER BEQUEATHED HIS COLLECTION OF RARE BOOKS and manuscripts to the Houghton Library in 1984, little to nothing was known about his MS Typ 299, a medieval chant manuscript that he had acquired in 1955. Subsequently identified as a fragmentary fourteenth-century antiphoner,[1] the manuscript has received little attention from scholars. It nevertheless turns out to be an exceptional manuscript, representing a rare—indeed, practically unique—liturgical innovation.

Fortunately, the source of the Houghton fragment survives in Gallarate, Italy: the twenty folios of MS Typ 299 originally formed part of MS M in the collection of the Archivio di Santa Maria Assunta. The liturgy conveyed by these two manuscripts combines the traditional Ambrosian liturgy and the monastic cursus found in Gregorian manuscripts—Ambrosian manuscripts typically do not contain elements of the monastic cursus. Furthermore, the melodic repertory of the manuscript includes traditional Ambrosian as well as Gregorian melodies.

Both the liturgical contents and aesthetic properties of the Houghton and Gallarate fragments connect them not only to each other but also to the only other Ambrosian manuscript that could be viewed as monastic. Rather than suggesting a substantial lost Ambrosian liturgical tradition, these close connections point to the innovations of a versatile and creative scribe: Antonius de Vomate.

MS Typ 299 contains chants for feasts of the *pars aestiva* of the Ambrosian liturgy. The manuscript was at some point disbound and rearranged: the folios are not in their correct liturgical order, and many feasts are incomplete. In the current arrangement, the most extensively decorated folio appears first. Figure 1.1 reconstructs the original order and codicological relationship of the extant folios. Table 1.1 gives the feasts in MS Typ 299 in their correct liturgical order.

---

1. Barbara Mahrenholz Wolff, *Music Manuscripts at Harvard: A Catalogue of Music Manuscripts from the 14th to the 20th Centuries in the Houghton Library and the Eda Kuhn Loeb Music Library* (Cambridge, Mass.: Harvard University Library, 1992).

fol. 9   fol. 14   fol. 19   fol. 13   fol. 11   fol. 10   fol. 1   fol. 8   fol. 12   fol. 20

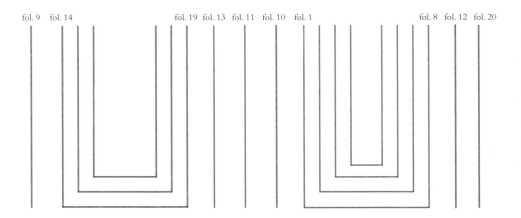

FIGURE 1.1   Cambridge, Mass., Harvard University, Houghton Library, MS Typ 299: reconstructed order and relationship of extant folios

Table 1.1. Feasts in MS Typ 299 in Liturgical Order

Feast	Date	Folio
Ascensio Domini		9r
Georgius	April 24	14r
Marcus	April 25	15r
Petrus martyr	April 29	15v
Philippus & Iacobus	May 1	16v
Inventio Sancte Crucis	May 3	16v
Victor	May 8	19v
Petrus & Paulus	June 29	13r
Nativitas Beate Marie Virginis	Sept. 8	11r
Cornelius & Cyprianus; Exaltatio Sancte Crucis	Sept. 14	11v
Eufimia	Sept. 16	10r
Satyrus	Sept. 17	10v
Mauritius	Sept. 22	1r
Michael	Sept. 29	6r
Sophya	Sept. 30	8v
Simon & Jude & Fides	Oct. 28	12
Sanctorum Omnium	Nov. 1	12v
Domenica I Post Pentec.		2r

Most of the liturgy in MS Typ 299 is typically Ambrosian. Mass corresponds exactly to what is found in other Ambrosian manuscripts. A close look at the night office, however, reveals that the manuscript does not follow a traditional Ambrosian liturgy throughout. The main deviations can be found in vespers and matins. First, MS Typ 299 does not contain the usual lucernarium at the beginning of vespers. Second, there is an invitatory antiphon at matins, which is also uncommon for Ambrosian manuscripts. Third, the first and second nocturns each include six psalms. Fourth, the third nocturn of matins has only one canticle antiphon. Finally, there are four instead of three readings with responsories for each nocturn.

While all five of these features are uncharacteristic of the Ambrosian rite, the last three are especially surprising since they point to monastic use, which is very rare in Ambrosian sources. Thus MS Typ 299 has a hybrid liturgy that contains both Ambrosian and monastic elements and was apparently produced for a community in the diocese of Milan. Monastic Ambrosian manuscripts are exceptionally rare[2] —only two known manuscripts have essentially the same hybrid liturgy. Michel Huglo identified a fourteenth-century antiphoner, thought to be from Viggiona and now in the Archivio Storico Diocesano in Novara (MS A 2), that exhibits a "rare example of a mixture of monastic use with the Ambrosian rite."[3] Huglo then connected the Novara codex to another Ambrosian manuscript with the same characteristics of hybrid liturgy. This other manuscript is the fragmentary antiphoner Gallarate M. We are now able to demonstrate that the Houghton fragment was once part of this Gallarate manuscript.

Comparison of the *mise-en-page* and scripts of the Houghton and Gallarate manuscripts supports this hypothesis (figs. 1.2 and 1.3). Both the Houghton and Gallarate fragments have folios ruled for nine lines, with a ruled space of approximately 25 × 16 cm. Each set of rules creates a system of four thin lines for musical notation and one wider line for script, with a total of forty-five lines per page. The scripts for both the noted chants and the cues are of the same scale and compression in each manuscript and employ the same repertory of letter forms.

Decoration of the two fragments is likewise very similar, if not in fact attributable to one hand. Although only MS Typ 299 has figural decoration, both manuscripts have a number of foliate initials with the same palette and decorative vocabulary of twirling leaves and knotted vines superimposed on a dark blue background with pen decoration in lead white. Such ornamental conventions are

---

2. Terence Bailey has commented that "no Ambrosian monastic antiphoner has been discovered; perhaps none was executed. It may be that Ambrosian monasteries (like so many ancient foundations on both sides of the Alps) were compelled, in the wake of the Frankish conquests and the reforms of Benedict of Aniane, to adopt the Benedictine Rule." Terence Bailey, "Ambrosian Chant," in *Grove Music Online*, ed. Laura Macy, http://www.grovemusic.com.

3. Michel Huglo, Luigi Agustoni, Eugène Cardine, and Ernesto Moneta Caglio, *Fonti e paleografia del canto ambrosiano*, Archivio Ambrosiano 7 (Milan, 1956), 228, no. 219.

FIGURE 1.2   Cambridge, Mass., Harvard University, Houghton Library, MS Typ 299, fol. 3r, 33 × 22

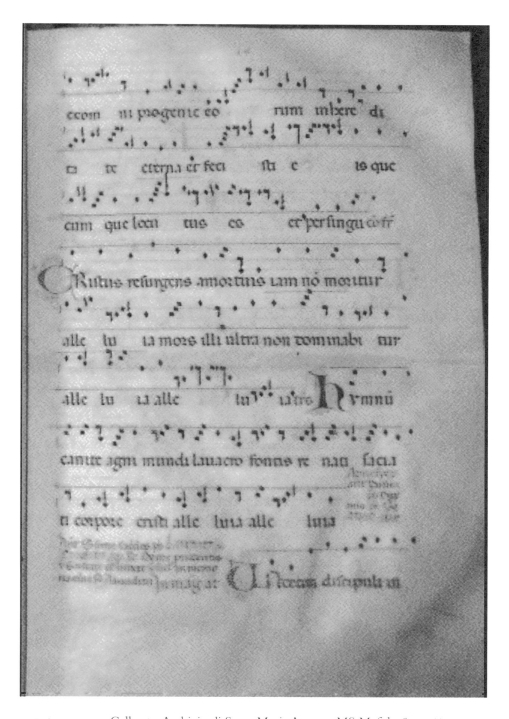

FIGURE 1.3   Gallarate, Archivio di Santa Maria Assunta, MS M, fol. 18r, 33 × 21.5

FIGURE I.4   Initial *A*s in Cambridge, Mass., Harvard University, Houghton
Library, MS Typ 299, fol. 9r, 24 × 21 (left) and Gallarate, Archivio di Santa
Maria Assunta, MS M, fol. 77r, 25 × 21 (right)

hardly uncommon in Lombard illumination of the period, but the two fragments
here build their initials out of a virtually identical set of basic forms. Two decorated
*A*s, for example, share the same essential design, and a similar combination of colors
(fig 1.4).

One example suffices to demonstrate the textual relationship between MS
Typ 299 and Gallarate M. In one opening from Gallarate M (fols. 33v–35r [the
manuscript is foliated discontinuously]), the left-hand page contains the introit
chant for the fifth Sunday after Easter, *Tanto tempore vobiscum*, ending with the words
"est alle[luia]"; the right-hand page begins with the antiphon *Elevata est magnificentia*
(fig. 1.5). The continuation of the introit chant is found on folio 9 of MS Typ 299.
Folio 9v of MS Typ 299 and folio 35r of Gallarate M are also continuous. Vespers
for the feast of the Ascension begins on folio 9 and concludes on folio 9v, where
it is followed by the beginning of matins. Note that the manuscript indicates an
antiphona super venite followed by the cue for its psalm. The continuation of matins
for Ascension can again be found in the Gallarate manuscript. On folio 35r there
are six antiphons, followed on fol. 35v by the four responsories for the four readings
of the first nocturn. The same is true for the second and third nocturns. Clearly the
two fragments once belonged to a single manuscript.

While a thorough investigation of the musical traditions reflected in these
manuscripts is beyond the scope of this essay, we can offer a few preliminary
observations concerning the origins of some of the chants. For matins of Ascension,
MS Typ 299/Gallarate M contains more responsories and antiphons than required
by the standard Ambrosian liturgy: fifteen and thirteen, respectively, instead of only

FIGURE 1.5   Gallarate, Archivio di Santa Maria Assunta, MS M, fols. 33v–35r (foliated discontinuously), 33 × 43

about three and nine (plus a few hymns). This raises the question of where the supernumerary chants for matins in our manuscript come from.

Table 1.2 compares the musical pieces for matins in the Ambrosian tradition, as represented in Oxford, Bodleian Library, MS Lat. liturg. a. 4, and the hybrid liturgy of MS Typ 299/Gallarate M. Pieces taken from the Ambrosian melodic tradition are printed in uppercase italics. For instance, the antiphon *Viri galilei*, for the second nocturn, contains a melodic section from the Ambrosian *antiphona ad crucem* for this feast. The second responsory and its verse for the readings of the second nocturn were taken from the Ambrosian vespers. This responsory, *Ascendens in altum*, also appears for vespers in our manuscript, where it is noted with exactly the same melody as in the Ambrosian tradition. The next responsory, *Excelsus super omnes gentes*, was taken over one-to-one from the *responsorium in baptisterium*. And finally, the *antiphona in cantemus Sedes tua Deus* appears to be the *antiphona in cantemus* from the Ambrosian rite.[4]

The Ambrosian borrowings in our manuscript account for only about 10–15 percent of all the musical pieces. Where did the other pieces come from? Since

4.   This antiphon is noted in vespers in MS Typ 299/Gallarate M and Lat. liturg. a. 4, and it corresponds to the version given in Terence Bailey and Paul Merkley, *The Antiphons of the Ambrosian Office* (Ottawa, Canada: Institute of Mediaeval Music, 1989) 224.

Table 1.2. Borrowings from the Ambrosian Tradition

Lat. liturg. a. 4

Ad Vesperas

Luc Quoniam **V** Quoniam in te
Ant in Choro Ascendens in altum captivam duxit
  (noted)
Hymnus Optatus votis omnium
R *ASCENDENS IN ALTUM* (noted)
  V REGNA TERRE (noted)
[...]

Ad Matutinum
R post hymn Benedicam **V** In Domino

Ant i De Nocte
Ant ii All. all.
Ant iii All. all. all.

R ad lec All. **V** Omnis terra
R ii All. **V** Pax multa

In Benedictus All. all. all. all.

Ad crucem *VIRI GALILEI QUID
  ADMIRAMINI ASPITIENTES* (noted)

In Cantemus *SEDES TUA DEUS*

In Benedicite Parata

In Laud Ascendit
Cap Cantate
Hym Optatus
R in bap *EXCELSUS SUPER OMNES
  GENTES* (noted) **V** *QUI SICUT
  DOMINUS* (noted)
al' psal Ascendo ad patrem meum (noted)

MS Typ 299/Gallarate M

Ad Matutinum
Ant super venite Alleluia regem ascendentem in
  celum (noted)

In 1 Nocturno
Ant Elevata est magnificentia (noted)
Ant Dominus in templo sancto suo (noted)
Ant A summo celo egressio Domini (noted)
Ant Exaltare domine in virtute tua (noted)
Ant Exaltabo te domine quoniam suscepisti me
  alleluia (noted)
Ant Nisi ego abiero paraclitus (noted)

Ad lectionem
R Alleluia **V** Ad te domine levavi
R Alleluia **V** Afferte domino
R Psallite deo **V** Lauda anima mea
R cum Gloria Elevata est magnificentia tua
  (noted) **V** Super celos Deus (noted)

In 2 Nocturno
Ant *VIRI GALILEI QUID ADMIRAMINI
  ASPITIENTES* (noted)
Ant Non turbetur con vestrum (noted)
Ant Nimis exaltatus est alleluia (noted)
Ant Pacem meam do vobis (noted)
Ant Dominus in syon (noted)
Ant Dominus in celo (noted)

Ad lectionem
R Laudabo dominum **V** Suavis
R *ASCENDENS IN ALTUM* **V** *REGNA
  TERRE*
R *EXCELSUS SUPER OMNES GENTES*
  (noted) **V** *QUI SICUT DOMINUS* (noted)
R cum Gloria A summo celo (noted) **V** Et
  occursus eius (noted)

In 3 Nocturno
In cant ant *SEDES TUA DEUS*

Ad lectionem
R Benedicam dominus **V** In domino laudabitur
R Alleluia **V** Omnis terra
R Alleluia **V** Pax multa diligentibus
R cum Gloria Exaltare domine in virtute tua
  (noted)
V Cantabimus et psallemus virtutes tuas (noted)

Table 1.3. Borrowings from the Gregorian Tradition

Lucca 601	MS Typ 299/Gallarate M
Matins	**Ad Matutinum**
Ad Invit ALLELUIA CHRISTUM DOMINUM ASCENDENNTEM IN CELUM (noted)	**Ant super venite ALLELUIA REGEM ASCENDENTEM IN CELUM** (noted)
In 1 Nocturno	**In 1 Nocturno**
Ant ELEVATA EST MAGNIFICENTIA (noted)	**Ant ELEVATA EST MAGNIFICENTIA** (noted)
Ant DOMINUS IN TEMPLO SANCTO SUO (noted)	**Ant DOMINUS IN TEMPLO SANCTO SUO** (noted)
Ant A SUMMO CELO EGRESSIO EIUS(noted)	**Ant A SUMMO CELO EGRESSIO DOMINI** (noted)
Ant EXALTARE DOMINE IN VIRTUTE TUA (noted)	**Ant EXALTARE DOMINE IN VIRTUTE TUA** (noted)
Ant Sic veniet quem (noted)	**Ant EXALTABO TE DOMINE QUONIAM SUSCEPISTI ME ALLELUIA** (noted)
Ant EXALTABO TE DOMINE(noted)	**Ant NISI EGO ABIERO PARACLITUS** (noted)
Ad lectionem	**Ad lectionem**
R Post passionem suam per dies (noted) **V** Et convescens (noted)	**R** Alleluia **V** Ad te Domine levavi
R Omnis pulchritudo **V** A summo celo (noted)	**R** Alleluia **V** Afferte Domino
R Exaltare domine alleluia **V** Cantabimus et psallemus	**R** Psallite deo **V** Lauda anima mea
R Si enim non abiero (noted) **V** Non enim loquetur (noted)	**R cum Gloria** Elevata est magnificentia tua (noted) **V** Super celos deus (noted)
In 2 Nocturno	**In 2 Nocturno**
Ant Rogabo patrem meum (noted)	Ant *VIRI GALILEI QUID* ADMIRAMINI *ASPITIENTES* (noted)
Ant Ascendit deus in iubilatione (noted)	**Ant NON TURBETUR CON VESTRUM** (noted)
Ant NISI EGO ABIERO (noted)	**Ant NIMIS EXALTATUS EST ALLELUIA** (noted)
Ant NIMIS EXALTATUS (noted)	**Ant PACEM MEAM DO VOBIS** (noted)
Ant DOMINUS IN SYON (noted)	**Ant DOMINUS IN SYON** (noted)
Ant DOMINUS IN CELO (noted)	**Ant DOMINUS IN CELO** (noted)
Ad lectionem	**Ad lectionem**
R Ascendit deus (noted) **V** Ascendens Christus in altum (noted)	**R** Laudabo dominum **V** Suavis
R Ascendens in altum (noted) **V** Ascendit Deus in iubilatione (noted)	**R** *ASCENDENS IN ALTUM* **V** *REGNA TERRE*
R Ego rogabo patrem (noted) **V** Si enim non habiero	**R** *EXCELSUS SUPER OMNES GENTES* (noted) **V** *QUI SICUT DOMINUS DEUS* (noted)
R Non conturbetur (noted) **V** Ego rogabo patrem (noted)	**R cum Gloria** A summo celo (noted) **V** Et occursus eius (noted)
In 3 Nocturno	**In 3 Nocturno**
Ant ad cantica Peter sancte serva cos in nomine tuo (noted)	In cant ant *SEDES TUA DEUS*
Ad lectionem	**Ad lectionem**
R Ponis nubem (noted) **V** Qui facis angelos (noted)	**R** Benedicam Dominus **V** In Domino laudabitur
R Non relinquam (noted) **V** Nisi ego abiero (noted)	**R** Alleluia **V** Omnis terra
R Tempus est (noted) **V** Pacem meam (noted)	**R** Alleluia **V** Pax multa diligentibus
R Viri galilei (noted) **V** Cumque intuerentur	**R cum Gloria** Exaltare domine in virtute tua (noted)
	V Cantabimus et psallemus virtutes tuas (noted)

MS Typ 299/Gallarate M, unlike most other known examples of Ambrosian chant, seems to be adapted for monastic use, we have also compared it to a manuscript from the Gregorian tradition. Table 1.3 compares our manuscript (with the Ambrosian repertory in uppercase italics) and Lucca, Biblioteca Capitolare, MS 601, a Gregorian antiphoner of the twelfth century, highlighting in uppercase bold those pieces in MS Typ 299/Gallarate M that were taken from the Gregorian tradition. It appears that two groups of antiphons (in addition to the invitatory antiphon) were imported from the Gregorian tradition: first, a group of six antiphons from the first nocturn, and second, a group of five antiphons from the second nocturn (in some cases the same melody was used for different texts).

A closer examination of the chants reveals that there is a high degree of similarity between the borrowed repertories. Example 1.1 shows the first antiphon in the first nocturn, *Elevata est magnificentia*. Below is the version as it appears in MS Typ 299/Gallarate M; above is the version from Lucca 601. A cursory comparison demonstrates that the melody has been transposed but otherwise remains essentially the same.

In the next antiphon in this group, *Dominus in templo sancto suo*, we find some slight variations between the two versions (ex. 1.2; again, below is the version as it appears in MS Typ 299/Gallarate M; above is the version from Lucca 601). In *A summo celo* there is also some slight variation, as there is in *Exaltare Domine in virtute tua*. *Exaltabo te Domine*, on the other hand, is virtually the same.

EXAMPLE 1.1

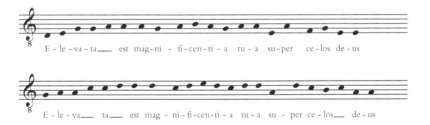

EXAMPLE 1.2

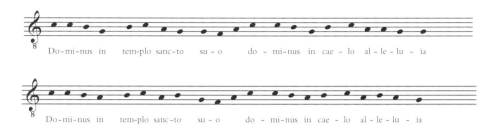

It appears that only antiphons were taken from the Gregorian repertory. This is surprising, because the main musical difference between matins in the Ambrosian and monastic offices is the higher number of responsories for the readings in the latter. One would therefore assume that in order to produce a manuscript with a hybrid liturgy, the scribe would have taken the Gregorian responsories as well. Where exactly the responsories for matins in MS Typ 299/Gallarate M come from remains to be seen. In fact, most of the responsories in this feast are not noted; it might well be that the responsories were also taken from the Gregorian tradition. It is remarkable, for instance, that the responsories *cum Gloria* in our manuscript have a very simple melody. Furthermore, in all three instances of the responsories *cum Gloria* the melody is exactly the same. Perhaps in this case the scribe could not find a good fit in the Ambrosian repertory. Did he invent his own simple melody, inserting it in the manuscript because he felt the Gregorian melodies were too elaborate and complicated?

A similar case occurs in the second group of antiphons imported from the Gregorian repertory, where all five Ambrosian antiphons—*Non turbetur, Nimis exaltatus* (see ex. 1.3), *Pacem meam, Dominus in Syon*, and *Dominum in celo*—have exactly the same melody. It seems that our scribe took the melody from the Gregorian tradition, where it appears in a group of antiphons (*Nimis exaltatus, Dominus in Syon*, and *Dominus in celo*), and used it for the antiphons in this group for which he did not yet have a suitable melody. All this seems to suggest that our scribe produced the manuscript in such a way that whenever he could rely on the Ambrosian repertory, he would take these melodies first, borrowing from the Gregorian repertory only in cases where he could not find Ambrosian melodies. As Matthew Mugmon has demonstrated, the borrowings from the Gregorian tradition are not limited to the feast of Ascension but appear in the feast of Saint Michael as well.[5] This further indicates not only that the liturgical structure of our manuscript

---

5.   Matthew Mugmon, "The Mystery of St. Michael: Gregorian Borrowing and Adaptation in MS Typ 299" (working paper, Department of Music, Harvard University, Cambridge, Mass., 2006).

is a hybrid of Ambrosian and Gregorian traditions but that the musical traditions were combined as well. Now that we have reunited Gallarate M and MS Typ 299, we have a much bigger pool of hybrid liturgical chants available to advance this research.

EXAMPLE 1.3

Ni-mis ex-al – ta-tus est al – le-lu-ia su – per om-nes de – os al-le-lu – ia

Finally, these distinctive elements of the MS Typ 299/Gallarate M manuscript invite some explanation of the book's origin and purpose. Where does it come from? Who made it? Who commissioned it, and for what community? The other Ambrosian monastic manuscript identified by Huglo, Novara A 2, may help answer these questions. The Novara codex contains the chants for winter; and although it is ruled differently than MS Typ 299/Gallarate M (eight rather than nine lines), its script and decoration strongly resemble those of our fragments (figs. 1.6 and 1.7).

The Novara manuscript includes two colophons; in the first, the scribe states that the book was commissioned by Andriola de Medici, professed at the monasterium novum, from Antonius de Vomate, beneficed at the Church of Santa Maria de Zippis. It cost a now-illegible number of gold florins. Antonius goes on to say, "scripsi notaui ligaui et superscripsi"; that is, he wrote, notated, bound, and rubricated the manuscript in the year 1360. The second colophon, written in the year 1360, again notes that the book was written and notated by Father Antonius de Gufredis de Vomate, beneficed at the Church of Santa Maria de Zippis. The close similarities in script and illumination between the Novara and the MS Typ 299/Gallarate M manuscripts—and, most important, the unique liturgy that only they share—strongly suggest that Antonius created the latter manuscript as well.

Evidently Antonius produced manuscripts for the convent in Milan associated with Santa Maria *ad, sub,* or *subtus* monasterium novum, which is documented as early as 1033 and survived until the suppression in 1798.[6] Proposing such a destination for MS Typ 299/Gallarate M, however, would not explain one of the manuscript's most striking artistic and liturgical features—the prominence accorded to Saint Mauritius. To explain this, we may have to look to another Milanese convent, also one of Antonius's monastic neighbors.

---

6.   Gualberto Vigotti, *La diocesi di Milano alla fine del secolo XIII: Chiese cittadine e pievi forensi nel "Liber sanctorum" di Goffredo da Bussero* (Rome: Edizioni di storia e letteratura, 1974), 73.

The importance of Saint Mauritius in MS Typ 299 is clear from the copious decoration provided for his feast. The manuscript's hierarchy of decoration accords some saints pen-flourished initials to begin their feasts, others small six- to eight-line decorated initials, and still others more elaborate ten- to twelve-line initials. An eleven-line, historiated initial opens the feast of the Holy Apostles Peter and Paul. A seventeen-line, historiated initial, extending into a full foliate border, in colors and gold, is provided for Saint Mauritius (fig. 1.8). Mauritius is clearly important in the Gallarate fragment as well: he appears in all but one of its twenty-seven litanies, and his name is the only one that always appears in red.

There was, of course, a great convent in Milan closely associated with Saint Mauritius, although it is now perhaps more famous for the Renaissance frescoes in its Chiesa di San Maurizio: the Monastero Maggiore, possibly the original destination for MS Typ 299/Gallarate M.

The little we know about our scribe Antonius may lend this hypothesis further support. According to his name, Antonius de Gufredis de Vomate came from the town now known as Omate, in the parish of Vilmercate (modern Vimercate). Omate was in fact controlled by the powerful Goffredi family,[7] of which Antonius's name also indicates he was a member. Two other books, both written in 1368, bear his signature and identify him as priest of the Church of Santa Maria in Circo: Milan, Archivio Sant'Ambrogio, MS M 24;[8] and Milan, Biblioteca Capitolare, MS II.E.1.22. Santa Maria al Circolo is mentioned in the *Liber notitiae sanctorum Mediolani*, attributed to Goffredo da Bussero, which was composed at the end of the thirteenth century.[9] It is just down the street from San Maurizio al Monastero Maggiore. Some association between the two places may be suggested by the reference to "Santa Maria ad circulum" in a litany on folio 66r of the Gallarate M fragment. We know that Antonius produced the Novara manuscript—the only other surviving Ambrosian monastic manuscript—for a patron from a neighboring female convent, Andriola de Medici of the *monasterium novum*. It therefore seems not unlikely that our manuscript originally had a similar destination. Antonius, the preliminary evidence suggests, produced these liturgical rarities for the use of local monastic foundations, for whom the combination of Milanese and monastic elements makes perfect sense.

7.   Francesco Bombognini and Carlo Redaelli, *Antiquario della diocesi di Milano* (Milan: G. Pirotta, 1828), 286.

8.   Huglo et al., *Fonti e paleografia*, 225, no. 129.

9.   Marco Magistretti and Ugo de Villard, eds., *Liber notitiae sanctorum Mediolani* (Milan: U. Allegretti, 1917), cols. 213 C, 233 C, 239 D, 248 C, 263 A; see also Gualberto Vigotti, *La diocesi di Milano alla fine del secolo XIII*, 32, 69.

FIGURE 1.6   Cambridge, Mass., Harvard University, Houghton Library, MS Typ 299, fol. 15v, 33 × 22

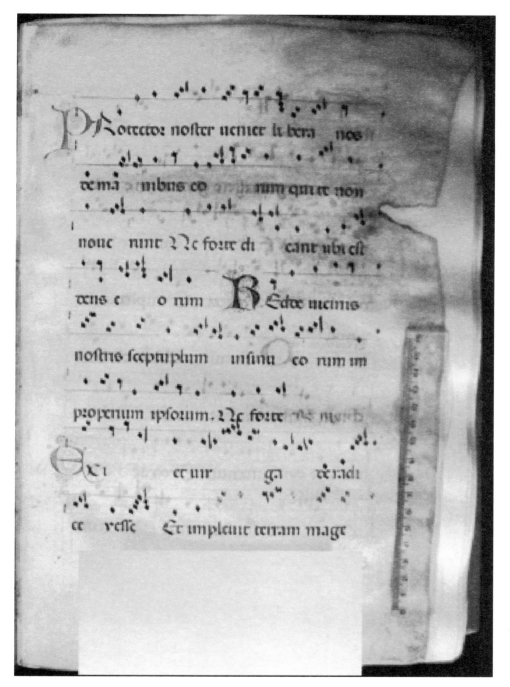

FIGURE 1.7   Novara, Archivio Storico Diocesano, MS A2, fol. 33r, 39 × 26

FIGURE 1.8   Cambridge, Mass., Harvard University, Houghton Library,
MS Typ 299, fol. 1r, 33 × 22

In addition to its importance for liturgical history, Antonius's production of these idiosyncratic manuscripts is of interest for the study of increasing professionalization and "mass-production" in the book trade of the later Middle Ages. In some ways, Antonius was indeed a professional, in that he produced books for institutions other than his own and charged for his services. But only some of the time: as he states in a rubric on the first folio of Milan MS II.E.1.22, "I made this book entirely at my own expense." He then begins, "donavi . . ." (I gave it), but the rest is illegible in natural light. This manuscript does not appear to incorporate the same monastic elements that occur in MS Typ 299/Gallarate M and the Novara manuscript, perhaps because he made it as a gift, and therefore possibly for a different kind of patron than those who commissioned the other manuscripts. His practice appears to have represented a kind of specialized professional production, distinguished by comprehensive individual craftsmanship rather than the division of labor. In particular, Antonius's claim in the Novara colophon to have bound the manuscript himself is unusual. He created manuscripts that were highly individual, if not unique, interpretations of the liturgy.

The authors thank Joseph Dyer, Thomas Forrest Kelly, and Matthew Mugmon for their assistance and helpful comments.

Long-lost Siblings?

Houghton's Summer Manuscript
and its Possible Counterpart

Matthew Mugmon

T HE MOST REVEALING FACET OF HOUGHTON LIBRARY MS LAT 389 may be its relationship to another source of Ambrosian chant. The antiphoner's eighty-four folios include much of the summer part of the Ambrosian liturgy as it was recorded in the late thirteenth or early fourteenth century. At first glance, aside from the fact that, in its present state, many folios are out of order and some parts of the liturgy and music are missing, the surviving material in MS Lat 389 is fairly standard.[1] Indeed, the manuscript offers few surprises when compared to more complete sources, such as the notated fourteenth-century manuscript Oxford, Bodleian Library, MS Lat. liturg. a. 4 or Marcus Magistretti's *Manuale Ambrosianum*,[2] recorded from an eleventh-century source.[3]

But another summer manuscript, Biblioteca Ambrosiana MS M 99 sup. (an almost complete summer portion produced in the same period as MS Lat 389)

---

1. The surviving portion of MS Lat 389 begins on Holy Saturday (in the manuscript's currently disordered state, fol. 70) and concludes during feria VI of the *commune feriarum* (fol. 79v). The book is missing folios throughout, including at the beginning and end. With the help of Terence Bailey and Giacomo Baroffio, as well as GianLuigi Rusconi and Giordano Monzio Compagnoni of the Pontifical Ambrosian Institute of Sacred Music, it was determined that this manuscript is indeed one of two that have previously been identified as having resided together in Varese and then in Milan. They are listed in Michel Huglo, Luigi Agustoni, Eugène Cardine, and Ernesto Moneta Caglio, *Fonti e paleografia del canto ambrosiana* (Milan, 1956), 251, no. 54, as having belonged to a Bianchi family, and Baroffio lists them as belonging to a "coll. Grassi" in Milan. See Baroffio, "Iter Liturgicum Ambrosianum: Inventario sommario di libri liturgici ambrosiani," *Aevum* 74 (2000): 583–603, available at http://spfm.unipv.it/baroffio/materiali/IterLitAmbr.rtf, which reflects the new identification. The other manuscript in this pair of "Grassi" books is Cambridge, Mass., Harvard University, Houghton Library, MS Lat 388, a twelfth-century winter manuscript.

2. Marcus Magistretti, ed., *Manuale Ambrosianum ex codice saec. XI* (Nendeln, Liechtenstein: Kraus Reprint, 1971).

3. Terence Bailey has noted that the "surviving copies of the [Ambrosian] antiphoner are in remarkable agreement and may have descended from a single archetype." "Ambrosian Chant," in *Grove Music Online*, ed. Laura Macy, http://www.grovemusic.com.

is so strikingly similar to MS Lat 389 as to suggest that the two may have been more than just independent witnesses to the same broad tradition. Indeed, their close relationship suggests the possibility that a single scribe produced both books, perhaps for the same church. To illustrate this, I first consider the clear physical similarities between the two manuscripts. I then explore liturgical issues by examining a specific feast as it appears in these two manuscripts with the same feast in Lat. liturg. a. 4. Finally, I evaluate some of the differences between the manuscripts and suggest areas for future research.

PHYSICAL SIMILARITIES

Details of paleography and layout shared by Ambrosiana M 99 sup.[4] and MS Lat 389 present compelling evidence that a single scribe may have created both. Elements such as letter forms and overall spacing are quite similar, and although the smaller initials are rarely, if ever, identical at corresponding points, they seem to depend on a common, limited set of choices for shapes and decorative touches (fig. 2.1).[5] Moreover, the more elaborate initials rely on a matching palette of filigree; the pen-and-ink *H*s shown in figure 2.2, for instance, adorn the same prominent feast in the two manuscripts. Finally, cues and rubrics are positioned comparably in relation to the notated texts (fig. 2.3). Similar examples abound.

CASE STUDY: THE BEHEADING OF SAINT JOHN THE BAPTIST

As an investigation of one feast shows, the liturgical organization of MS Lat 389 matches that in Ambrosiana M 99 sup., even where MS Lat 389 differs from other sources. Rowland Moseley has compared the layout of the feast of the Beheading of Saint John the Baptist as it appears in MS Lat 389 with two other sources—the summer portion from Lat. liturg. a. 4 and the *Manuale*.[6] Moseley found several cases in which, despite a general agreement of these three witnesses, the order of specific pieces sometimes differs. In these cases, Ambrosiana M 99 sup. agrees with MS Lat 389 almost exactly.

The layout of vespers in MS Lat 389 and Lat. liturg. a. 4 is nearly the same,

---

4. References to this manuscript cite the modern foliation written in the upper right margins.

5. The images of manuscripts in this article are sized to facilitate comparison. Several differences between the manuscripts are discussed below, but it is worth noting here that the staff lines are closer together in MS Lat 389, which contains twelve lines of text and music per page compared to the nine in Ambrosiana M 99 sup. Moreover, MS Lat 389 leaves no space between those lines, unlike Ambrosiana M 99 sup. Also, the writing area of MS Lat 389, at 23 × 16 cm, is slightly larger than that of Ambrosiana M 99 sup., whose writing area measures 22 × 15 cm.

6. Rowland Moseley, "Variations on Ambrosian Themes" (working paper, Department of Music, Harvard University, Cambridge, Mass., 2006).

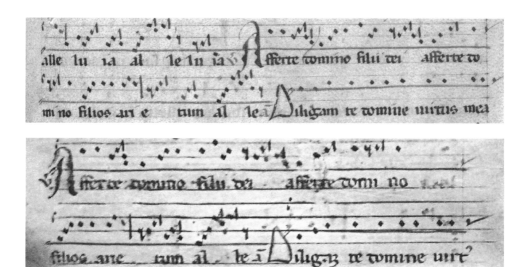

FIGURE 2.1   Cambridge, Mass., Harvard University, Houghton Library,
MS Lat 389, fol. 66r, detail, 4 × 17 (above); Milan, Biblioteca Ambrosiana,
MS M 99 sup., fol. 17v, detail, 5 × 16 (below)

 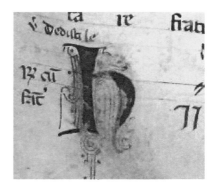

FIGURE 2.2   Opening initial of responsory *Hi sunt, qui secuti* for saints
Protasius and Gervasius, in Cambridge, Mass., Harvard University, Houghton
Library, MS Lat 389, fol. 38v, 7 × 5 (left); Milan, Biblioteca Ambrosiana,
MS M 99 sup., fol 63v, 6 × 8 (right)

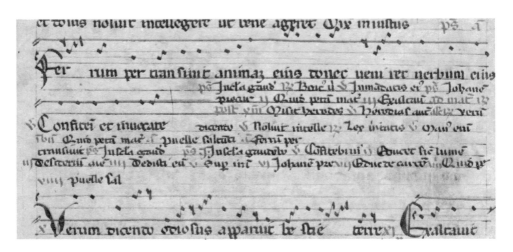

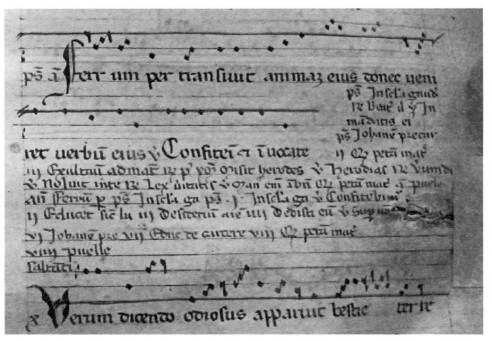

FIGURE 2.3   Cambridge, Mass., Harvard University, Houghton Library,
MS Lat 389, fol. 60v, detail, 8 × 17 (above); Milan, Biblioteca Ambrosiana,
MS M 99 sup., fol. 100r, detail, 11 × 15 (below)

and it is only partway through vigils, as seen in table 2.1, that differences in the existence or ordering of pieces appear.[7] MS Lat 389 (H) contains an additional notated antiphon—*Verba oris eius* (fol. 60v)—and a cued responsory. Neither of these elements appears at that point in Lat. liturg. a. 4 (Ox), but both exist in the *Manuale* (Mn) at that point. Interestingly, both pieces also appear in Ambrosiana M 99 sup. (fol. 100).

Table 2.1. Feast of the Beheading of Saint John the Baptist: Opening Portion of Vigils (after Moseley, "Variations on Ambrosian Themes")

Item	Mn	M99	H	Ox
R. Misit herodes	~	•	•	•
V. Herodias autem	~	•	•	•
Ant. Educ de carcere	~	~	~	~
ps. Voce mea	~	~	~	~
R. Lex veritatis	~	~	~	~
V. Manus enim	~	~	~	~
Ant. Verba oris eius	~	•	•	
ps. Dixit iniustus	~	•	•	
R. Verum dicendo	~	~	~	
V. Noluit intelligere	~	~	~	
Ant. Ferrum pertransivit	~	•	•	•
ps. Confitemini Domino	~	•	•	•

KEY: • = includes notation; ~ = text-only cue

This departure from Lat. liturg. a. 4 does not mean, however, that MS Lat 389 and Ambrosiana M 99 sup. differ from Lat. liturg. a. 4 only by agreeing with the *Manuale*. As seen in table 2.2, the order of pieces in the *mane* section of the feast in MS Lat 389 agrees with Ambrosiana M 99 sup. but disagrees with the other sources, including the *Manuale*. This detail is especially striking because in both Ambrosiana M 99 sup. and MS Lat 389, the section consists of eleven psallendae, labeled by roman numerals, appearing in exactly the same order, with the first nine

---

7. Except for the final two rows of table 2.1, material in the table for MS Lat 389 and Ambrosiana M 99 does not appear in figure 2.3 above. The cues in table 2.2 for those manuscripts, however, are visible in figures 2.3.

cued and the final two notated in each manuscript. The order and layout do not correspond precisely to those in the *Manuale* or Lat. liturg. a. 4, even though in this case the order in Amb M 99 sup. and MS Lat 389 is closer to that of the *Manuale* than to that of Lat. liturg. a. 4. Given the usual slight variation that has already been observed among the generally similar sources of the Ambrosian summer portion, one would expect manuscripts to match in the way Ambrosiana M 99 sup. and MS Lat 389 do only if their origins were closely linked.

**Table 2.2. Feast of the Beheading of Saint John the Baptist: *Psallendae in mane*
(after Moseley, "Variations on Ambrosian Themes")**

Item Text	*Mn*	*M99*	*H*	*Ox*
In saecula gaudebo	1	1	1	
Confitebimur [verse]	~	~	~	
Educet sicut lumen	2	2	2	2
Desiderium animae	3	3	3	
Dedisti eum	4	4	4	
Super iram	5	5	5	
Desiderabiliora	6			1
Iohannem praecursorem	7	6	6	2•
Educ de carcere	8	7	7	4
Quid petam	9	8	8	5
Puellae saltanti	10	9	9	6
Verum dicendo	11	10•	10•	3•
Ferrum pertransivit	12			7
Verba mea				8
Verba oris eius	13			
Exaltavit Dominus caput	14	11•	11•	P•

KEY: • = includes notation; ~ = text-only cue;
1, 2, etc. = labeled order of psallendae (~ implied unless otherwise noted);
P = labeled "post Kyrie cum Gloria"

Finally, in matins, the antiphon *Quid petam*, for the Benedicite, precedes *Puellae saltanti*, for the Benedictus in MS Lat 389 and Ambrosiana M 99 sup. The *Manuale* and Lat. liturg. a. 4, however, list the Benedictus antiphon first—in the order that has been noted as correct for this feast and others in the Ambrosian liturgy.[8] Even if the ordering of antiphons in MS Lat 389 and Ambrosiana M 99 sup. is simply a mistake, the common error underscores their shared history.

Differences between
Ambrosiana M 99 sup. and MS Lat 389

Although Ambrosiana M 99 sup. and MS Lat 389 are not identical, the overall similarities overwhelm the plentiful but minor musical and scribal differences between the two. Indeed, the small scale of these variations further supports the hypothesis that one scribe was responsible for both. One would expect two manuscripts that are not exact copies of each other—but that are still closely related—to exhibit differences.

Returning to the feast for the beheading of John the Baptist, the antiphon *Verba oris eius*, absent from the feast in Lat. liturg. a. 4, is notated in Ambrosiana M 99 sup. (fol. 100) a fourth below the pitch level at which it is written in MS Lat 389 (fol. 60v). The interval content, however, remains the same between the two manuscripts. That the pieces are notated at different pitches suggests that direct copying, either between manuscripts or from an exemplar, was not necessarily involved, at least at this particular point in the sources. And that the general positioning of cues is similar may still result from a single scribe's—or tradition's—ideas about layout carrying over from one manuscript to the other.

Notated cues for psalm tones may also differ among the summer manuscripts. The psalm tone of the final psallenda of vespers on folio 99v of Ambrosiana M 99 sup. is identical to the one at the corresponding point in Lat. liturg. a. 4 (fol. 198), but it differs from the one in MS Lat 389 (fol. 60). Lest one conclude that Biblioteca Ambrosiana M 99 sup. always corresponds to Lat. liturg. a. 4 when it digresses from MS Lat 389, the psalm tone for the cued *Confitemini [Domino] et invocate*, in vigils, is different in each manuscript, but the version in MS Lat 389 (fol. 60v) appears to be closer than the one in Ambrosiana M 99 sup. (fol. 100) to the one in Lat. liturg. a. 4 (fol. 198v). (See fig. 2.3 to compare this psalm tone in MS Lat 389 and Ambrosiana M 99 sup.) Variation in the choice of a psalm tone seems conceivable even in two closely related sources. But a large-scale study comparing these details across the three manuscripts would reveal whether or not patterns exist and whether they have implications for these manuscripts' origins.

---

8. Terence Bailey and Paul Merkley, *The Antiphons of the Ambrosian Office* (Ottawa, Canada: Institute of Mediaeval Music, 1989) 129.

In figures 2.1, a musical disagreement occurs between the manuscripts on the final syllable of "Afferte," where an additional A–B figure appears in MS Lat 389 that is missing in Ambrosiana M 99 sup. Here again, a more detailed study of specific sections of the sources is necessary to evaluate fully such small but noticeable musical variations, which again suggest that although the manuscripts likely shared a scribe, material was not directly copied from one manuscript to the other through a mechanical visual process.

For a possibly more significant musical difference, this time in the minor Dedication feast, *Fundamenta eius*, the opening *antiphona in choro*, is notated in MS Lat 389 (fol. 5) a fourth below its notation in Ambrosiana M 99 sup. (fol. 113v). Some internal locations, as well as the ends of the chants, are not identical. And in this case, B-flats would be needed in the version of Ambrosiana M 99 sup. to keep the interval content of this antiphon the same between that source and MS Lat 389 in the sections of the chants that do correspond. But no B-flats are notated in this piece in Ambrosiana M 99 sup. The necessary flats appear in Lat. liturg. a. 4 in this chant, which closely matches the Ambrosiana M 99 sup. version. Flats were thus conceivably understood for, if not written in, Ambrosiana M 99 sup. More study is necessary, but potentially significant musical differences between Ambrosiana M 99 sup. and MS Lat 389, such as this one, seem to be unusual. Their investigation, alongside close examinations of other manuscripts' versions, may ultimately shed more light on the relationships between these manuscripts and the development of the Ambrosian tradition.

Although the placement of cued and notated items corresponds closely in Ambrosiana M 99 sup. and MS Lat 389, the manuscripts are not identical in this respect. For example, *Quam beata mors sanctorum*, in the Mass for Saint Mauritius, is written out and fully notated in MS Lat 389 (fol. 23) but only cued in Ambrosiana M 99 sup. (fol. 104v).[9] It is perhaps more telling that these two manuscripts agree in labeling the piece as an alternative offertory ("al") instead of as a transitorium— its label in Lat. liturg. a. 4. Disagreements such as these, then, are not prominent enough to derail a sense that Ambrosiana M 99 sup. and MS Lat 389 have scribal connections.

Finally, there are also minor differences in the spellings and abbreviations used in the two manuscripts. Even if the same scribe produced both, some variation was

---

9. In the surviving parts of both manuscripts that do correspond, there are instances in which rubrics and cues that exist in one manuscript—often Ambrosiana M 99—are not present in the other. For example, a large set of rubrics and cues for the Nativity of the Blessed Virgin Mary appears in the margins of folio 101 of Ambrosiana M 99. These cues do not exist in MS Lat 389, which makes no mention of the feast, and were likely added to Ambrosiana M 99 after the manuscript was first produced. Also deserving of further study in Ambrosiana M 99 are portions of the manuscript, previously identified as added material, that begin on folio 202. See Michel Huglo et al., *Fonti e paleografia*, 48, no. 57.

bound to occur; the small disagreements in orthography may simply bear witness to a scribe engaged in the task of creating books, not in making exact reproductions. The overwhelming agreement of the manuscripts in the smallest liturgical details indicates that both were, in sum, destined for use in the same local tradition.

NEXT STEPS

Even in the context of the overall agreement among manuscripts of Ambrosian chant, the similarities between the two sources under consideration here suggest that they may have been written at the same place and possibly for the same church. Further study may even reveal the minor scribal and musical differences as points in the development of parts of the Ambrosian liturgy. Unfortunately, although identifying information in one of the manuscripts might shed light on the provenance of the other, such information is scarce. An inscription on folio 201 of Ambrosiana M 99 sup., however, does seem to offer a possible name, "Magister Cefinus," as the scribe.[10]

More telling information, however, is not forthcoming. Material on the inside cover of Ambrosiana M 99 sup., on folio 1, and on folio 201v mentions "S. Sepulchro," "S. Sepulcri," and "Sancti Sepulchri," respectively. But these references only confirm that the manuscript resided for a time at San Sepolcro, a church near the Biblioteca Ambrosiana in Milan, not that it necessarily originated there.

Even though the exact provenance of Ambrosiana M 99 sup. and MS Lat 389 is unknown, the established similarities between the two may allow us to investigate them both jointly and to draw significant conclusions about one from studying the other. Although at this stage, any contrasts between them seem too inconsistent to place one before or after the other, more research into the kinds of differences described above—and further comparisons of these sources with others —may eventually reveal one to be the younger or older sibling. And this kind of progress could in turn lead to more insights into the historical development and transmission of Ambrosian chant.

I wish to thank Thomas Forrest Kelly for his generous assistance throughout the preparation of this paper, the members of a Harvard seminar on Ambrosian

---

10.   Huglo et al., *Fonti e paleografia,* 48, no. 57. Here, the text is transcribed as, "Deo gratias. Qui fecit hoc opus magister ceFinus no(m)i(n)e dici(tur)."

chant for providing me with copies of their work, Monsignor Marco Navoni at the Biblioteca Ambrosiana in Milan, and the students with whom I visited the Biblioteca Ambrosiana. Moreover, I would like to thank Mirella Ferrari for communicating with me on the similarities between the two manuscripts discussed in this paper. I also had fruitful conversations with Terence Bailey and Angelo Rusconi.

In Defense of Green Lines,

or

The Notation of B-flat in
Early Ambrosian Antiphoners

Anna Zayaruznaya

T HE GREEN LINES with which this study concerns itself have already achieved a certain notoriety among scholars of Ambrosian chant. They appear in hundreds of passages in the British Library Add. MS 34209, the twelfth-century antiphoner long considered to be the earliest surviving redaction of music for the winter part of the Ambrosian liturgy.[1] To some, these lines may be more familiar as the thick gray marks in the facsimile reproduction of the manuscript in volume 5 of *Paléographie musicale*. Whether green or gray, the lines hover in the space where B should be, and are clearly meant to indicate B-flat (see fig. 3.1, where the green lines appear a fourth above red staff lines labeled with F clefs at points where the melody would otherwise be outlining tritones).

What is less clear, however, is the origin of these lines. Are they part of the initial notation for the manuscript or the addition of a later hand? Reacting to their color and quality, Michel Huglo judged them to be much later: "Una lineetta orizzontale verde fu aggiunta molto tardivamente per significare il *si* bemolle, ma quest'aggiunta è sovente incerta e contradditoria."[2] The editors of *Paléographie musicale* were also rather severe in their estimation of the marks, judging them to be the work of incompetent scribes or uninformed musicians.[3]

---

1. For a detailed description, see Michel Huglo, Luigi Agustoni, Eugène Cardine, and Ernesto Moneta Caglio, *Fonti e paleografia del canto ambrosiano*, Archivio Ambrosiano 7 (Milan, 1956). Cataloged in Giacomo Baroffio, *Iter Liturgicum Italicum* (Padua: Cleup, 1999), 104; and Baroffio, "Iter Liturgicum Ambrosianum: Inventario sommario di libri liturgici ambrosiani," *Aevum* 74 (2000): 585.

2. Huglo et al., *Fonti e paleografia*, 41, no. 50.

3. "Dans le manuscrit original une main très postérieure a tracé grossièrement un trait vert sur un grand nombre de *si*. L'auteur de ces adjonctions a-t-il voulu *bémoliser* cette note? Nous serions portés à le croire, si ces *bémolisations* n'étaient pas faites le plus souvent d'une manière maladroite. Elles révèleraient, en tout cas, une ignorance complète de la tonalité ancienne, & s'écarteraient des indications tansmises par d'autres documents ambrosiens." *Paléographie musicale* 6,

33

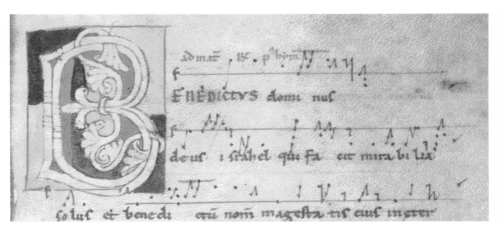

FIGURE 3.1   Green B-flat lines in London, British Library, Add. MS 34209, fol. 51r (p. 101), 5 × 11

Recent scholarship has been somewhat more kind to the green lines. Rembert Weakland warns that it is "not clear on what grounds [scholars] have judged that this line was added much later," calling the chronology of the green ink "a thorny issue in transcribing and studying Ambrosian chants."[4] Terence Bailey has also taken the lines more seriously, arguing that they are used intentionally in some passages in the manuscript and omitted consistently in others.[5] Thus while he does not weigh in on their authenticity, Bailey admits the lines as valid evidence of some particular state of the chant. Missing from all studies, however, is any thorough paleographical or codicological examination of the marks in question.

There is indeed cause for confusion about the green lines. At times they seem to have been added casually—even sloppily, compared to the rest of the notation. And the strangeness of the color green—otherwise largely absent from the notation of music—doesn't help. Finally, the very notion that B-flats would be indicated with such precision and consistency in a twelfth-century Italian manuscript goes against our expectations. Indeed, this last objection has been the most serious. The consensus is that "other manuscripts of the twelfth century . . . are generally without the written B flat."[6]

Antiphonarium Ambrosianum du Musée Britannique (XIIe siècle) Codex Additional 34209 (1896–1900; repr., Berne: Lang, 1971), 26.

4.   Rembert Weakland, "The Office Antiphons of the Ambrosian Chant" (Ph.D. diss., Columbia University, 2000), 292–293.

5.   Terence Bailey, *The Transitoria of the Ambrosian Mass: Compositional Process in Ecclesiastical Chant*, vol. 79, Wissenschaftliche Abhandlungen (Ottawa, Canada: Institute of Mediaeval Music, 2003), 17.

6.   Weakland, "The Office Antiphons of the Ambrosian Chant," 292–293.

How are we to accept the green lines as authentic, given the silence of other twelfth-century sources? And if Add. 34209 notates B-flat, why don't other early sources do so? This seems especially perplexing in light of the fact that the practice of signing B-flat is common in thirteenth-century Ambrosian manuscripts.[7]

In fact, the silence of sources may be a result of our not listening carefully enough. While no other manuscript contains green lines indicating B-flat, a survey of the other three surviving twelfth-century sources for the winter half reveals a variety of notational methods for indicating the problematic semitone. It is worth briefly considering each manuscript.[8]

The only one of the four sources to survive complete (or nearly so), and probably the latest of the group, is Milan, Biblioteca Capitolare, II.F.2.2.[9] As Weakland observes, the manuscript does not notate B-flats.[10] However, I argue below that it does in fact contain comparable scribal evidence that helps us shed light on the green lines in Add. 34209.

The next source, Biblioteca Apostolica Vaticana Vat. lat. 12932, is the most fragmentary of the four, containing only twenty folios.[11] Yet even this relatively small number of folios reveals many examples of signed B-flat. Although I have not been able to examine the manuscript in person and cannot comment on the ink of the flat signs, close scrutiny of the available facsimiles gives no reason to doubt the originality of the marks (see fig. 3.2), whose presence becomes all the more significant when considered in light of the other three contemporaneous Ambrosian sources.

Finally, and perhaps most significantly, the recently acquired twelfth-century winter antiphoner now known as Houghton Library MS Lat 388 brings a new perspective to the issue.[12] I have found that several passages in this manuscript

---

7. Ibid., 292.

8. This study concerns itself with the winter part of the liturgy because more of these manuscripts have survived from the twelfth century than witnesses for the summer part.

9. The dating of this source, also called the *Codex Metropolitanus*, is somewhat in question. Huglo notes that although Don Garbagnati has assigned it to the middle of the twelfth century, paleographic evidence argues for the end of that century. Terence Bailey also lists it as belonging to the twelfth century, while Giacomo Baroffio gives it to the thirteenth. See Huglo et al., *Fonti e paleografia*, 46–47, nos. 55–56; Bailey, *The Transitoria of the Ambrosian Mass: Compositional Process in Ecclesiastical Chant*, xi; and Baroffio, "Iter Liturgicum Ambrosianum," 584.

10. Weakland, "The Office Antiphons of the Ambrosian Chant," 292–293.

11. Cataloged in Huglo et al., *Fonti e paleografia*, 268; Baroffio, "Iter Liturgicum Ambrosianum"; and Baroffio, *Iter Liturgicum Italicum*, 287.

12. This manuscript is cataloged as "Varese, Bianchi" in Huglo et al., *Fonti e paleografia*, 46, no. 53. Baroffio lists it as "Milano, Coll. Grassi (già?)" in his "Iter Liturgicum Ambrosianum: Inventario sommario di libri liturgici ambrosiani," *Aevum* 74 (2000): 587. In an updated online version of this inventory Baroffio identifies MS Lat 388 as "Milano, olim Coll. Grassi (olim Varese Bianchi)." (spfm.unipv.it/baroffio/materiali/IterLitAmbr.rtf).

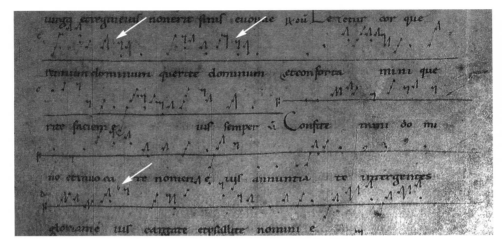

FIGURE 3.2   Signed B-flats in Vatican City, Biblioteca Apostolica Vaticana,
Vat. lat. 12932, fol. 16r

contain a red line a fourth above F—at B, or rather, as the tritones outlined by the
passages in figure 3.3 would suggest, at B-flat.[13] Overall there are seven places in MS
Lat 388 where B-flat seems to be indicated by red lines, and these together mark
some sixteen notes. The scale, then, is not nearly akin to that of the green lines in
Add. 34209, but the phenomenon of marking B-flat with a colored line is the same.

Significantly, all B-flats marked in red in MS Lat 388 are also marked, in
green, in Add. 34209. Furthermore, there is no indication that the red lines of MS
Lat 388 might be later: here, ink and style match. This circumstance, combined
with the evidence of Vat. lat. 12932, calls for a careful look at B-flat lines in these
sources, whether red or green, and ultimately demands that we think more broadly
about the processes of addition and edition in the creation of early Ambrosian
antiphoners.

CLEFS AND LINES IN AMBROSIAN MANUSCRIPTS

All four manuscripts under consideration use the system of cleffing introduced by
Guido of Arezzo. In addition to letters that act as clefs, Guido recommended that
colored lines be used to indicate the pitches of staff lines: red for F and yellow for
C. Ambrosian manuscripts do indeed follow these guidelines, but I suggest that
we nuance the terminology slightly to admit of two kinds of colored lines, which
I will call *axis lines* and *reference lines*. The *axis line* is a line that is drawn regardless

---

13. My interpretation of these lines agrees with Moneta's reading of a similar passage in Varese,
     Sacro Monte, jemale A. Cited in Huglo, *Fonti e paleografia*, 224, no. 65.

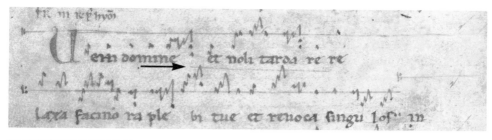

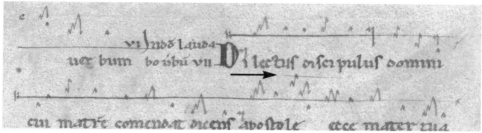

FIGURE 3.3   Red B-flat lines in Cambridge, Mass., Harvard University,
Houghton Library, MS Lat 388, fol. 44v, 4 × 16 (above), and fol. 64r, 4 × 14
(below)

of whether or not its pitch is sung. For instance, in the top line of figure 3.4, the
F never sounds but the F axis line is present. The axis line can indicate either an F
(red) or a C (yellow), and when the chant is located in and around the pitch-space
between F and C, both lines are present. However, when the chant has only C as
an axis line, the F line is drawn as necessary, for reference, when the chant goes up
to F. I will refer to these shorter lines, which play the part of ledger lines within
the two-line Guidonian staff, as *reference lines*.[14] Most reference lines are red lines
on F, and their function is to remind us that a half-step is located between the line
and the note beneath it. B-flat lines could, by this definition, be extensions of the
cleffing system—a B-flat reference line, like the one on F, warns of the half-step
below.

This is how we ought to understand the red lines in MS Lat 388 and,
indeed, the green lines in Add. 34209. But while the former seem indigenous to
their surroundings, the color of the latter gives pause: why do they have to be
green? While green seems like a strange choice, we should remember that, after
red and yellow, it was the most common colored pigment available to scribes, and
many eleventh- and twelfth-century manuscripts use these three colors in their

---

14.   A further distinction between axis and reference lines is that the former are almost always on
      a dry-point line, which adds to their stability. Reference lines, on the other hand, may be in
      spaces. When this rule is broken, mistakes are made, as in MS Lat 388, folio 110.

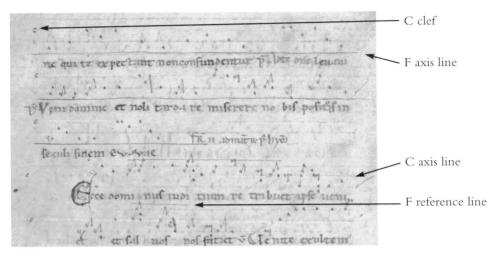

FIGURE 3.4   Cleffing in Ambrosian manuscripts: Cambridge, Mass., Harvard University, Houghton Library, MS Lat 388, fol. 43v, 10 × 16

decorations.[15] In some cases, it seems, green may even have been more available than yellow: the makers of a twelfth-century troper-proser from Saint-Évroult chose to use green, rather than yellow, for C lines.[16] However, pigments are not all created equal, and colored inks especially can have idiosyncratic effects on the parchment to which they are applied. In the London manuscript, the lines seem like outsiders because they are thick and seem haphazardly applied to a manuscript that is otherwise carefully executed. But this seeming haphazardness has to do with the nature of the green ink: in many places, the pigment has bled through the parchment or spread, leading to wider lines in the process (fig. 3.5). Indeed, where the green lines have not bled, they look almost as careful as the red lines that surround them (as in fig. 3.1).

15.   For example, see the full-page illustration on folio 39v of the eleventh-century gradual of Santa Cecilia in Trastevere, reproduced in color in Max Lütolf, ed., *Das Graduale von Santa Cecilia in Trastevere (Cod. Bodmer 74)*, Biblioteca Bodmeriana 2 (Cologny-Genève: Fondation Martin Bodmer, 1987).

16.   Paris, Bibliothèque nationale de France, MS lat. 10508. For a reproduction, see Heinrich Besseler, Max Schneider, Werner Bachmann, and Bruno Stäblein, *Musikgeschichte in Bildern*, Band 3, *Musik des Mittelalters und der Renaissance*, Lieferung 4, *Schriftbild der einstimmigen Musik* (Leipzig: Deutscher Verlag für Musik, 1975), 119. Stäblein says that the green line and the red F line were both "nachgefärbt," but I believe that the findings presented below may call for a reevaluation of this claim. I am grateful to Joseph Dyer for bringing this source to my attention.

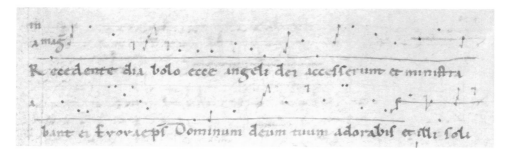

FIGURE 3.5   Bleed-through of green lines in London, British Library, Add.
MS 34209, fol. 75v (p. 150), 3 × 11

The pigment in question is verdigris, a manufactured copper acetate that was popular in book and panel painting throughout the Middle Ages. While the ink must have appealed to artists because of its lightfastness and attractive blue-green hue, it is notorious for its instability and corrosive qualities, its tendency to bleed through parchment, and its unpredictability:

> Sometimes it has corroded the parchment, eaten into it, so that
> the painted parts actually drop out and leave gaps in the page: and
> sometimes it has behaved quite quietly, and stayed in place, and kept
> its transparent blue-green color without any of these distressing
> accompaniments. . . . The accidents of time affect no other pigment so
> generally or so disastrously as verdigris.[17]

A similar bleed-through process can be observed in another Houghton manuscript, an eleventh-century leaf from a Beneventan missal (MS Typ 701, fig. 3.6). Here, it might also be tempting to call the mess created by verdigris bleed-through a "later" addition, but it is clearly integrated into the design of the page: the pigment highlights the beginning of each sentence and adds definition to the bovine evangelist at bottom left.[18]

Returning to Add. 34209, we can make one more observation: the green of the decorated initials and that of the green lines is the same hue. True, the pigment looks more opaque in some of the backgrounds to initials, but this is in part due to concentration of paint: while the green of the B-flat lines is meant to be transparent, so as not to obscure the notes it modifies, color added to initials is

---

17. Daniel V. Thompson, *The Materials and Techniques of Medieval Painting* (New York: Dover Publications, 1956), 165–166.

18. Significant bleed-through can also be observed in the Saint-Évroult manuscript—see note 16, above.

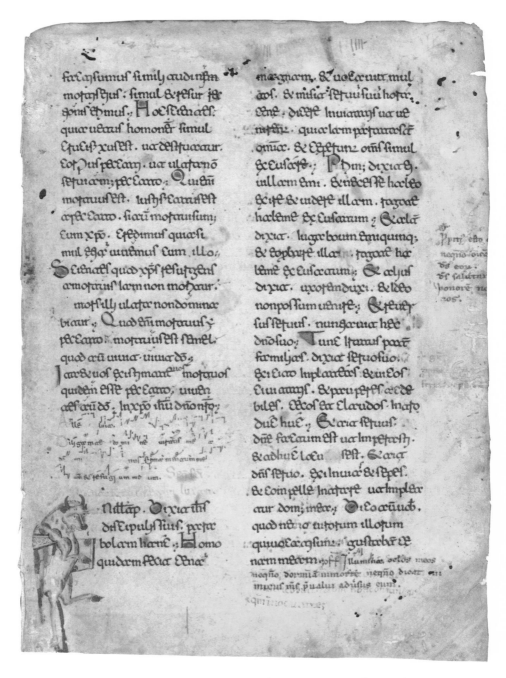

FIGURE 3.6 Cambridge, Mass., Harvard University, Houghton Library, MS Typ 701, 36 × 25

meant to be bold. A decorated *O* on folio 76 uses a more diluted form of the pigment, maybe because its animal subject matter calls for depiction rather than decoration (fig. 3.7). Here we can easily observe the identity of hue between the illumination and the B-flat reference lines.

FIGURE 3.7   London, British Library, Add. MS 34209, fols. 75v–76r (pp. 150–151), 5 × 7

Another indication that the green pigment used for the decoration of initials could be transparent as well as opaque comes from an unfortunate *C* on folio 89v of Add. 34209, which boasts green polka dots on a yellow background (fig. 3.8). In this example, it is easy to see that the yellow background of the *C* matches the *C* axis lines, while the green of the polka dots matches the B-flat lines.[19] Even for verdigris, the dots here seem to have bled quite a bit, which suggests that the yellow background may still have been wet when the green was applied. This in turn raises questions about the knowledge and ability of the manuscript's scribes when it came to decoration. It seems likely that pigment was applied not by artists but by music and/or text scribes, and that we might be mistaking for carelessness or

---

19.   The red of the initial's border seems to match that of the rubrication and probably that of the F axis lines.

later vandalism something that is in fact a messiness resulting from inexperience—a point to which I return below. For now, we may simply note the identity in hue between the colored initials and the green lines. The possibility that the B-flat pigment may in fact have come from the same pot of ink as the dragon and the polka dots strengthens the suggestion that green reference lines were part of the original design of the manuscript.

FIGURE 3.8   London, British Library, Add. MS 34209, fol. 89v (p. 178), 5 × 10

The affinity in color between decorated initials and green B-flat reference lines also suggests that the lines might have been applied at the same time as color to the initials. But is it possible that the initials too were colored by a much later hand? In fact, could all color, whether green, red, or yellow, be a later addition to Add. 34209?

There are indeed documented cases of lines having been added to chant manuscripts by later hands. A case in point, and a relatively local one, is the addition of colored lines to Benevento, Biblioteca Capitolare, MS 38. Thomas Forrest Kelly has noted that red F lines there were added, probably in the thirteenth century, to those chants still being sung.[20] However, the analogue to Add. 34209 is not exact. Beneventan notation was older and less disposed to Guidonian innovations. Milanese notation, on the other hand, exists only on staves and "seems to have

---

20. Thomas Forrest Kelly, *Paléographie musicale* 21, *Les témoins manuscrits du chant Bénéventain* (Solesmes: Abbaye Saint-Pierre, 1992), 349–350, 52–53.

been newly created at the time when the staff was introduced."[21] Still, the question remains, are axis and reference lines later additions to Ambrosian manuscripts, or do they represent a part of the original scribal plan? Here again, MS Lat 388 provides some compelling answers.

THE CASE OF THE MISSING RED LINES

On five folios of MS Lat 388 red lines—whether axis or reference—are entirely missing. Four of these fall on complete openings (80v–81r and 83v–84r) and the fifth, folio 78v, faces a folio whose red lines begin a third of the way down the page and are different in quality and color from the others in the gathering, strongly suggesting addition at a separate stage. Thus there are three openings on which the scribe(s) initially neglected to draw F lines (one of these is reproduced as fig. 3.9).

On the face of it, such lacunae would suggest that axis and reference lines are indeed a later addition to MS Lat 388. However, several important details about the omission should be noted. First, all openings missing red lines are found in gathering 11 of the manuscript.[22] Encompassing folios 77–84, this is the last gathering written by the first of two main scribal hands in the manuscript. It is possible that this particular gathering was rushed, perhaps by whatever circumstance necessitated the change of hand in the first place. Or perhaps the reverse is true—that the change of hand was necessitated by the carelessness of the initial scribe(s). Certainly, the portion of the book written by the smaller hand, which takes over on folio 84r, is not subject to the kinds of corrections evident in the first half of the manuscript. Thus the transition seems likely to be from a less to a more experienced scribe— perhaps from student to teacher. If so, we may view the lack of red axis lines as a final straw.

Furthermore, although red lines are missing, yellow axis lines are present on these folios.[23] The openings thus cannot support the lateness of all colored lines. Even more significant is a series of irregularities in rubrication and in the drawing

---

21. Though Kelly's contribution to this volume suggests that Ambrosian notation may be older than previously suspected. For the received view, see David Hiley and Janka Szendrei, "Notation, §Iii, 1(V): Plainchant: Pitch-Specific Notations, 11th–12th Centuries: (D) North Italy, Including Milan," in *The New Grove Dictionary of Music and Musicians*, ed. Stanley Sadie (London: Macmillan, 2001), 189.

22. I am grateful to Ryan Bañagale for his detailed codicological examination of MS Lat 388.

23. Due to its light color, it is difficult to speculate about whether yellow has been added under or over the notes, but indirect evidence suggests that the former may have been the case. For instance, folio 9r has a passage in which a yellow reference line has been drawn in but not used; such a mistake could hardly have been made after the chant had been notated. Additionally, the stopping points of yellow lines tend to be less controlled than those of red; on two adjacent systems of folio 10v, yellow axis lines continue several inches past clef changes that make them obsolete.

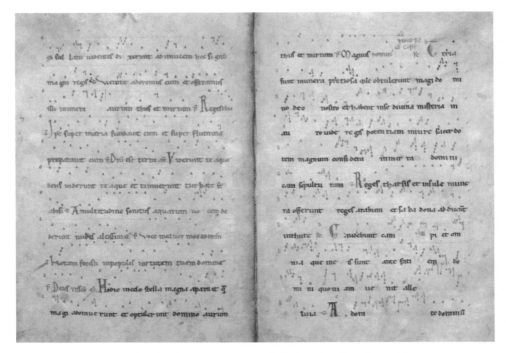

FIGURE 3.9   Cambridge, Mass., Harvard University, Houghton Library,
MS Lat 388, fols. 80v–81r, 25 × 35

of majuscule initials that would normally be red. On folios 80v–81r, for instance, the red ink is smudged and uneven, and possibly of several hues. Folio 83v is even more telling: here, a red hand has twice traced over brown rubrication—once for the responsory *Viderunt*, and again for the verse *Inluxerunt* (fig. 3.10). In both cases, the original brown rubrication was correct in its genre designation, but incorrect in its color, since rubrication is in red throughout MS Lat 388 and within the wider manuscript corpus. The *V* in *Viderunt* is also drawn by an incongruous and shaky hand in a space that had been left for a red majuscule incipit.[24] A similar situation exists on folio 78v, where a darker brown rubric and a brown letter *S* in a clearly different hand replace the rubric "cañt," and the *S* in *Super flumina*—a letter that should certainly have been red because it heads the first item of a mass (fig. 3.11).[25]

In short, much of what should be red on those folia missing F lines was in fact written awkwardly in brown and only sometimes retraced in red. And those red rubrications that are not tracings appear to be drawn on top of erasures—again, very likely erasures of text erring in color rather than content. The inescapable

---

24. We know that the letter should have been red because "responsoria ad lectio" and "cum infantibus" (this one is both) generally begin with red initials; compare folio 88.

25. Compare the red initial of the ingressa *In conspectu* (fol. 76).

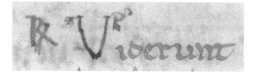 

FIGURE 3.10   Initials of responsory *Viderunt*, 1 × 3.5 (left) and verse *Inluxerunt*, 1.5 × 4 (right): Cambridge, Mass., Harvard University, Houghton Library, MS Lat 388, fol. 83v

conclusion is that folios 78v, 80v, 81, 83v, and 84 were at one stage missing not only their F lines but also any trace of red ink. This suggests that the F lines, rubrication, and red majuscule letters were (at least in this case) part of a single copying stage. The only other possible conclusion—that these folia were skipped during rubrication and then coincidentally skipped again some years later when red F lines were added—is highly improbable. We must assume then that red lines are original to the manuscript and that their omission is as unnatural as would be the antiphon *Uper flumina Babylonis*—not disastrous, since we know to supply the S, but certainly not intentional.

The haphazard approach to axis and reference lines demonstrated by the lacunae in the eleventh gathering is by no means typical of MS Lat 388. Though the unit of omission there is the opening, elsewhere in the manuscript there is every indication that axis lines were drawn with care, often separately for each piece.[26] The lines were even subject to correction: on folio 50, mistakenly drawn-in red lines are crossed out, and new ones added.

One other fact connected with cleffing remains to be mentioned, and this has to do with the layering of inks. Even a cursory glance at MS Lat 388 reveals that the manuscript has been subject to many corrections, additions, and re-tracings

FIGURE 3.11   Cambridge, Mass., Harvard University, Houghton Library, MS Lat 388, fol. 78v, 4 × 15

---

26. See, for example, *Letamini* (fol. 57).

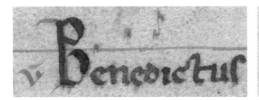 

FIGURE 3.12   Red Lines drawn on top of light-brown ink in Cambridge, Mass., Harvard University, Houghton Library, MS Lat 388, details of fol. 4r, 1.5 × 3 (left) and fol. 83r, 1.5 × 3.5 (right)

by darker inks. One obvious explanation is that the light brown ink in which the manuscript was originally written faded with time, necessitating tracing with darker pigments. However, the layering of red lines and corrections does not support such a hypothesis. Most red lines lie on top of the lighter brown layer of notes and under the darker correcting hand, as might be expected (fig. 3.12). But there are several exceptions—places where red lines are drawn *over* the correcting ink. Folio 64v defies analysis in having both versions in quick succession—a passage where red ink is layered over the corrections, and another in which corrections clearly appear to be overlaying red ink (fig. 3.13). In fact, there are exceptions to almost any claim that can be made about the layering of inks in this manuscript, leading to the strong possibility that the first layers of correction (the tracings over with dark ink) were correctives not to ink that had faded with time but to ink that was too light to begin with (perhaps another sign of the initial scribe's inexperience or extreme age). Writing out and proofreading were two consecutive or nearly consecutive steps in the creation of MS Lat 388.

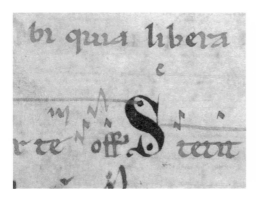 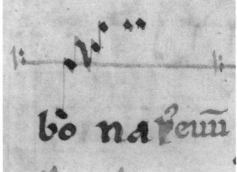

FIGURE 3.13   Ink layering in Cambridge, Mass., Harvard University, Houghton Library, MS Lat 388: red ink over corrections on fol. 64v, 3 × 4 (left); corrections over red ink on fol. 64v, 2.5 × 3 (right)

STAGES OF ADD. 34209

For Add. 34209, it is also possible to show that the red lines were added at an intermediate stage in the manuscript's creation. A detail on folio 51r shows that the red axis lines were put in after the illuminated capitals were drawn but before they were colored in (see fig. 3.1). Here, the scribe has allowed the F axis line above "solus" to dictate the bottom border of the initial, which seemingly skips the clef, becomes a red F line, and ends in a custos and an A clef. Because of this, the yellow background on the left half of the initial ends lower than the purple background on the right. The example also implies that the intricate *B* was drawn before notation was added, since the A clef is superimposed upon it: surely the artist could have avoided the clef if it had been there first.

This moment suggests a likely order of operations for the creation of the manuscript. First, the text was written and illuminated letters were drawn but not yet colored. Second, notation was added. Third, red ink was applied, including rubrication, the red borders of initials, and F lines. Fourth, yellow ink was applied, including decorations and C lines. Finally, the other colors used in the decoration of initials were applied in turn, and green lines were painted in. The last stage was not a terribly artistic process, as evidenced by the sloppy application of paint to many of the illuminated initials (including those in figs. 3.7 and 3.8). Indeed, as I have suggested, the application of color to the letters may well have been done by a music scribe—a possibility that would explain the messiness of the backgrounds when compared with the neat letters that they enhance.

The final pages of Add. 34209 argue most eloquently against the late addition of green lines (or of any lines, for that matter) to the manuscript. Starting with folio 134v, extra material is added to the manuscript in six stages, each of which has its own ruling practices, script, and set of inks. In the responsory *Venite exultemus*, red F axis lines are consistently used (fig. 3.14, region A). The next piece, *Desiderabiliora sunt*, is written by a smaller hand and in a darker ink, with no F or C lines (fig. 3.14, region B). Next come two alleluias that use red F lines (fig. 3.14, region C, continued in fig. 3.15, region A).

The next alleluia again uses no axis lines of any sort (fig. 3.15, region B). The following one, in a large and messy hand, uses red and yellow lines, and fills in the two A's of *Alleluia* with yellow paint (fig. 3.15, region C). On the last page, a large but controlled hand uses no red or yellow lines—in fact, no color at all (not pictured). No one drew in green lines on these final pieces, nor did they even supply uncontroversial red F lines. In short, we have no evidence for the later addition of colored lines to this manuscript.

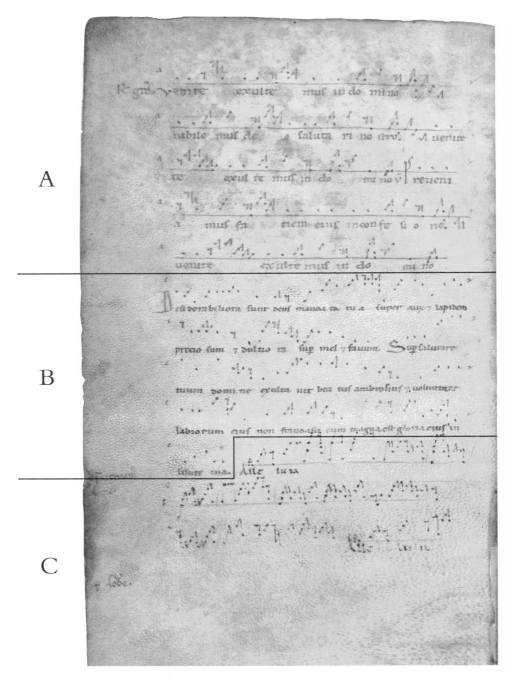

FIGURE 3.14   London, British Library, Add. MS 34209, fol. 134v (p. 268), 22 × 14

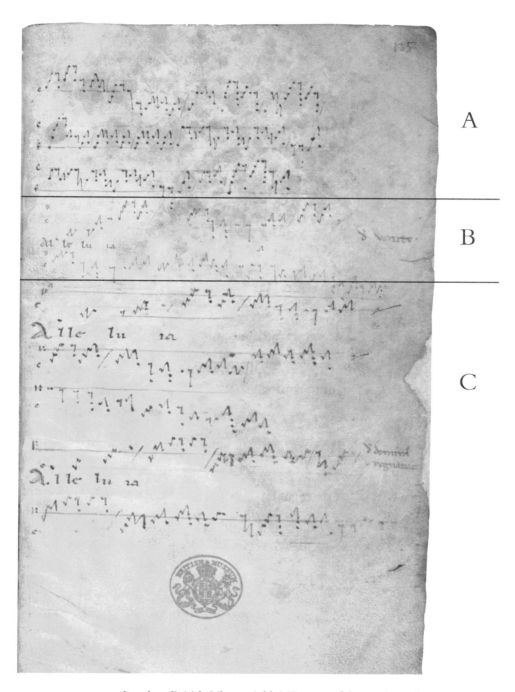

FIGURE 3.15   London, British Library, Add. MS 34209, fol. 135r (p. 269), 22 × 13

PROOFREADING WITH COLOR

One final observation strengthens the case for the early addition of green lines to Add. 34209 while simultaneously raising the much broader issue of their purpose. So far, discussions of the green ink have been limited to B-flat lines. However, in at least one case its purview extends to the neumes themselves: on folio 62v, two forgotten Gs set to the word "dei" have been written in green ink (fig. 3.16). The edition in *Paléographie musicale* includes these notes without remark, perhaps because the editor was partly relying on a black-and-white film. Clearly the two notes are supposed to be there: a clef change exists after them in order to accommodate them, and the custos on the previous line points to G. Furthermore, the reading of two Gs on "dei" is confirmed by MS Lat 388 (fig. 3.17). In this case, then, the person writing with green ink in Add. 34209 has acted as a proofreader. The antiphon is not complete in the London manuscript without its green notes.

Strange as the use of a cleffing ink for proofreading might seem, there is in fact an analog to this practice in Milan II.F.2.2. In this manuscript too scribes used colored ink both to indicate and to correct pitch. While most clefs here, as in Add. 34209 and MS Lat 388, are written in the same brown ink as the notes, twenty-two folios contain C clefs drawn in red ink. Sometimes, these clefs were added in

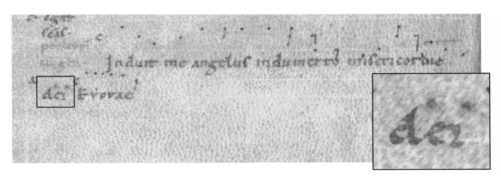

FIGURE 3.16   London, British Library, Add. MS 34209, fol. 62v (p. 124), 3 × 10

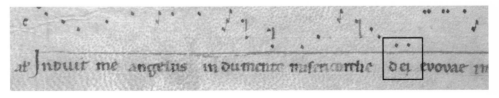

FIGURE 3.17   Cambridge, Mass., Harvard University, Houghton Library, MS Lat 388, fol. 91r, 2 × 13

red simply because there was no clef present.[27] Like the green Gs on "dei" in Add. 34209, the editor is here supplying missing content with whatever ink color he happens to have in his hand. But in other cases the hand wielding red ink actually changes the clef, and these changes are always from F to C (as in figs. 3.18 and 3.19). In figure 3.18, the clef change may be a simple correction, since the custos of the previous system indicates that the first note of the next system should be a D, not the G that would have resulted from the original clef.[28] However, the change in the passage shown in figure 3.19, along with many others in the manuscript, is musically motivated.

Let us focus on a single piece, the responsory *Ecce Dominus dominator* (fig. 3.20). In Milan II.F.2.2, the F clef on the second system has been changed to a C clef by a red hand, with the result that what would have been a B-flat on "altisimi" [*sic*] is now an F. The opening of the piece also uses a red reference line on "Dominus," implying that the clef at the beginning of the system is no longer

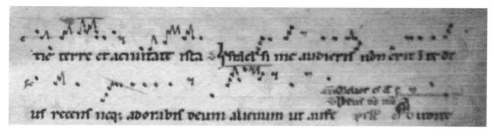

FIGURE 3.18   Milan, Biblioteca Capitolare, II.F.2.2, fol. 76r, 4 × 14

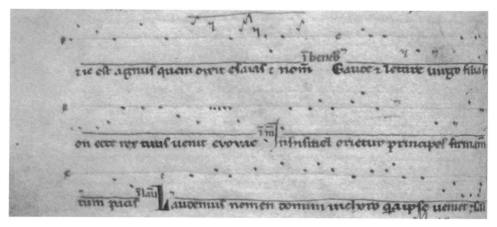

FIGURE 3.19   Milan, Biblioteca Capitolare, II.F.2.2, fol. 33v, 7 × 16

27. As on folio 36.

28. The same passage in MS Lat 388 is transmitted with a C clef throughout.

in effect. Clearly the proofreader noticed a problem with the original notation while adding red lines to the manuscript during a late stage of its production. That problem was the melodic tritone on "Dominus," and the solution was to switch the clef from F to C, automatically converting every B to an F.

In Add. 34209 the problem is solved in a different way. Allowing the F clef to stand, the scribe added his usual green B-flat line (gray in the reproduction in fig. 3.20). Interestingly, MS Lat 388 also uses an F clef and a B-flat reference line at this point (fig. 3.20, bottom image), though the lack of F axis line in the top system makes it look more like the re-cleffing in Milan II.F.2.2. However, there is an F clef to the left of "Ecce," and the corresponding custos is true to that clef.

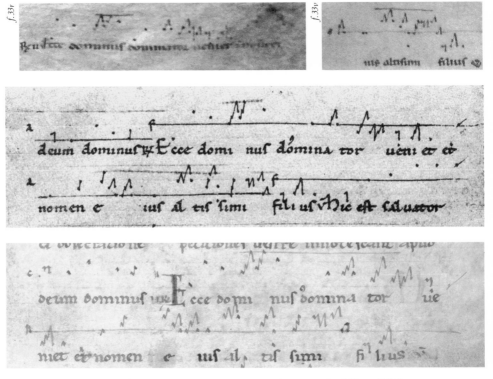

FIGURE 3.20 The responsory *Ecce Dominus dominator* in Milan, Biblioteca Capitolare, II.F.2.2, fol. 33r–v, 3 × 13/3 × 7 (above); in London, British Library, Add. MS 34209, fol. 23r (p. 45), 3 × 11 (middle); and in Cambridge, Mass., Harvard University, Houghton Library, MS Lat 388, fol. 44r, 4 × 16 (below)

Comparison of this passage across three manuscripts shows that each scribe's approach is essentially the same: with a colored ink used primarily for drawing axis and reference lines, they engage in an act of musical proofreading to change the offending tritone into a fourth.

What is interesting here is not only that each source shows evidence of steps taken to correct or clarify a difficult passage but that in each case the corrections can be dated—based on the various paleographical observations presented above—close to the manuscript's initial creation. The red Cs of Milan II.F.2.2, the green lines of Add. 34209, and the red lines of MS Lat 388 are not the work of "une main très postérieure"; rather, they were drawn in by a hand only slightly later than that which wrote the notes.

I would suggest that there is a difference in kind, and not just in degree, in scribal corrections that are part of a manuscript's initial copying, and those that are entered in by later, unconnected hands. Changes made later in the history of a manuscript may suggest changes in the ways of singing or in repertory or the atrophy of memorial archives and increased dependence on written music. On the other hand, if these lines are original to the mid-twelfth century, we can get a coherent idea of the repertory at the time of this manuscript's creation. Pinning down this chronology allows us to make more sense of the complicated collection of interdependent markings that constitutes this nine-hundred-year-old object. It also reminds us that the original makers of these books did not leave it to later ages to add specificity or increase accuracy: they did their own work, and the marks of their editors need not be read as hands from the future disciplining the texts of the past.

The Editor as Musician

An inquiry into the layering of inks in sources that are nearly nine hundred years old may seem self-indulgent, but the issues raised by this investigation of scribal roles take us beyond the page and into the mind of the scribe at a particular moment. Can we hear his thoughts? By way of concluding, I would like to dwell a little on the process of adding these clefs and reference lines in the context of medieval reading practices.

Recent studies of premodern literacy have greatly enhanced our understanding of how medieval readers interacted with their texts. It is clear that reading was, until the late Middle Ages, an oral and aural process.[29] Often it was done in groups, and when text manuscripts were copied, the process was one of dictation rather than silent transcription. Thomas Aquinas made notes for himself

---

29. Paul Henry Saenger, *Space between Words: The Origins of Silent Reading*, Figurae, Reading Medieval Culture (Stanford, Calif.: Stanford University Press, 1997). This may not have been the case in antiquity, however. See M. F. Burnyeat, "Postscript on Silent Reading," *Classical Quarterly* 47, no. 1 (1997): 74–76. The view stemmed from studies of literacy in classical antiquity and was later extended into the Middle Ages and sometimes even as late as the seventeenth century. A. K. Gavrilov summarizes the history of the idea for classical studies in "Techniques of Reading in Classical Antiquity," *Classical Quarterly* 47, no. 1 (1997), 56–57.

and then dictated to his secretaries,[30] and as a young man Augustine famously puzzled when he saw Saint Ambrose reading silently.[31] Perhaps, Augustine suggests, Ambrose did not want to be interrupted by requests to explain some obscure passage in his readings. "Besides, the need to preserve his voice, which used easily to become hoarse, could have been a very fair reason for silent reading."[32] Reading— at least a certain, common kind of reading—could make one's voice tired, and we can imagine medieval libraries as buzzing with murmurs well into the twelfth century, before gradually falling silent.

Manuscript copying too changed over the course of the High Middle Ages. Paul Saenger notes that a "transition from oral to visual modes of book production" was already underway in the twelfth century, when there are accounts of copyists working *in silentio*.[33] The result of this more visual mode of copying was that texts could be transmitted without comprehension, and Petrarch commented pejoratively about scribes who were mere "painters" because they copied texts by sight without understanding them.[34]

But if copying text was on its way to being a silent process in the scholastic atmosphere, it seems that the copying of music lagged slightly behind—neumatic notation was, after all, still a relatively new alphabet at the beginning of the twelfth century. Elizabeth Eva Leach locates the shift to a "mechanical, visually based copying" of music to the late Middle Ages, citing John of Tewkesbury's 1351 complaint that "all the *notatores* are not singers nor scribes: they are clerks, in truth they are painters."[35]

---

30. Mary Carruthers, *The Book of Memory: A Study of Memory in Medieval Culture*, Cambridge Studies in Medieval Literature 10 (Cambridge: Cambridge University Press, 1992), 4.

31. This passage has been traditionally read as Augustine's first encounter with silent reading; for a more nuanced view that diminishes its importance as evidence for the rarity of silent reading, see Gavrilov, "Techniques of Reading in Classical Antiquity," 61–66.

32. Augustine, *Confessions*, trans. Henry Chadwick, Oxford World's Classics (Oxford: Oxford University Press, 1991), 93.

33. Saenger, *Space between Words*, 252.

34. Even later Jean Gerson would echo this complaint; ibid.

35. "Omnes notatores non sunt cantores, nec scriptores sunt clerici, vere, pictores enim sunt"—the statement is a response to poor coordination of syllables and notes; Elizabeth Eva Leach, *Sung Birds: Music, Nature, and Poetry in the Later Middle Ages* (Ithaca: Cornell University Press, 2007), 113. There is also some manuscript evidence of "mechanical" music copying in the fourteenth century. As Friedrich Ludwig first noted, the Machaut manuscript B is a copy of the source Vg "qui s'efforce de reproduire exactement l'original," to the extent of precisely replicating gathering structure, page layout, and line-ends. "La musique des intermèdes lyriques dans le Remède de Fortune," in Ernest Hoepffner, *Oeuvres de Guillaume de Machaut*, vol. 2 (Paris: Firmin-Didot, 1911), 408–409. As Margaret Bent has since shown, such "careful" copying may well have been a result of ignorance on the part of the scribe, who indifferently aligned music and text, and in some cases copied the notes from one piece over the words to another; "The Machaut Manuscripts Vg, B and E," *Musica Disciplina* 37 (1983): 56–57.

This complaint about music scribes serves as useful evidence of an earlier norm that was being breached: *notatores* should be singers since musical literacy would improve their product. And it is hard to imagine the twelfth-century copyists of Add. 34209 as anything other than scribe-singers creating books for their own use or the use of nearby communities. The very defects of their work—inelegant script, clumsy decorations, crooked lines—hint that their expertise was perhaps to be found elsewhere.

Musical expertise would also act as a time-saver. If copying is to be a mechanical process that involves the eyes only, the neume becomes an abstract shape that must be redrawn exactly. But such a method would take much longer: any music scribe, especially one familiar with the repertory he copied, would surely let his voice aid him. Thus a scribe copying chant would very likely be at least humming along, and perhaps fully singing the chant as he wrote—and then again as made corrections and added colored staff lines.

Not all aspects of manuscript copying are equally musical: there is little question that red F axis lines could be added mechanically. I invite my reader to mentally add red lines to MS Lat 388, folio 81 (the right half of fig. 3.9). All that is necessary is to locate the F clefs and extend a line to the right of them until a new clef is given (usually at the beginning of a new piece). Yellow lines would be added in the same way, but with the scribe using C clefs as his guides. In both cases, a ruler, a pen, and a medium level of attention could get the job done.

However, other kinds of corrections would have required full musical concentration. Chief among these was the "thorny" question of B-flat, answered in Add. 34209 by every green line, or by its absence. The "sloppy" lines are perhaps rather just rushed, because they are taking place in real time. And whereas a ruler can be used to draw an axis line, these short reference lines must have been drawn freehand, to connect only those notes on the page that need to be flattened.

When we see these lines, then, we are in a sense seeing a performance. We might even get some insight into phrasing as well as pitch. Consider, for instance, the passage from Add. 34209 reproduced as figure 3.21. Here, we see two green

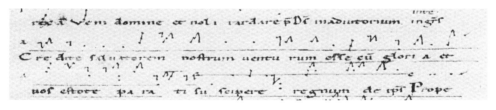

FIGURE 3.21   London, British Library, Add. MS 34209, fol. 19r (p. 37), 3 × 13

lines indicating B-flat that could have been made in one stroke, but were not. Why? I think it likely that our scribe drew as he sang, or sang as he drew. Thus the sometimes sloppy lines of the London manuscript are not an artistic but a musical act—at once proofreading and prescribing; asking and answering in real time that difficult question, How do we sing this note?

———◆———

I am grateful to Thomas Forrest Kelly for his comments on several drafts of this project and to Joseph Dyer for his careful reading and critique of the present text. I am indebted to Sarah Adams of the Isham Library for ordering materials for my research.

Ambrosian Chant:

New Manuscripts and New Problems

Angelo Rusconi

THIS ESSAY PRESENTS SOME "NEW" SOURCES OF AMBROSIAN CHANT and proposes that, for the first time, careful research be undertaken on the later tradition of this repertory and especially the Renaissance sources that transmit it.

For some time, the "archaeological" perspective on the study of Gregorian chant—although treated by some as the only valid one—has been considered too narrow. The evidence that liturgical chant has developed over time, always changing in a dialectical relationship between preservation and innovation, between respect for the past and attention to new needs and tastes, cannot be neglected. If the restoration of old melodies is one acceptable mode of investigation, one may also study musical and liturgical sources using other methods, considering these sources as important keys to our knowledge of the historical and cultural periods to which they bear witness.

The Renaissance is an interesting period in the history of liturgical plainchant. The close connection between ecclesiastical demands and new cultural norms suggests fruitful research questions on the entire period, not just those that relate to the Council of Trent. The starting point of this research is always connected with church life, but at the same time a contemporary humanistic mode of thought is strongly evident. Authors criticize the "barbaric" style of many liturgical texts (for example, the hymns). Some remarks directly address the relationship between music and words, and such remarks are also found in music theory treatises. The recurrent issue is the way in which music corresponds to short and long, or stressed and unstressed, syllables in the text. This issue concerns not only the recitative passages, but also the placement of melismatic passages. Theorists discuss issues such as melodic structure, modal rules, and notation. Their vocabulary and ideas fully align with classicist ideals of the period, favoring order and clarity. Manuscripts and printed plainchant books, then, clearly show the influence of this new Renaissance culture. Later, we further recognize the specific traces left by the Counter-Reformation.

Studies and facsimile editions of liturgical chant books published after the Council of Trent are important to musicologists. Among these is the famous *Editio*

Medicea.[1] In addition to the official Roman editions, scholars have studied other books promoted by publishers and by those who have revised chant materials on their own initiative, such as the *Graduale* edited by Orazio Vecchi, Andrea Gabrieli, and Ludovico Balbi (Venice, 1591).[2] Some attention has been devoted to local reforms of liturgical chant, such as that connected with Saint Barbara at Mantua or that of the so-called patriarchino rite at Como.[3]

In this large area of musicological and historical research, there is an astonishing omission: the tradition of the important center of Milan. While some subjects in this period, such as experiments in Tridentine polyphony, have been studied, the liturgical chant of the Milanese church, commonly called Ambrosian chant, has been ignored. A bibliography on later sources of Ambrosian chant is almost nonexistent.[4]

1. *Graduale de Tempore iuxta Ritum Sacrosanctae Romanae Ecclesiae: Editio Princeps (1614)*, ed. Giacomo Baroffio and Manlio Sodi; and *Graduale de Sanctis iuxta Ritum Sacrosanctae Romanae Ecclesiae: Editio Princeps (1614/15)*, ed. Giacomo Baroffio and Eun Ju Kim, with Manlio Sodi, Monumenta Studia Instrumenta Liturgica 10–11 (Vatican: Libreria Editrice Vaticana, 2001). Baroffio analyzes revised melodies in "La trasmissione delle melodie gregoriane nell'Editio Medicea e nelle fonti parallele," *Polifonie* 6, no. 2 (2006): 11–41 (English translation: "The transmission of Gregorian melodies in the Editio Medicea and in the parallel sources," 43–52). Angelo Rusconi considers theoretical issues in "La revisione delle melodie gregoriane nei teorici del XVI secolo," *Polifonie* 5, no. 3 (2005): 151–163 (English translation: "The revision of gregorian melodies in the 16th-century theorists," 165–177).

2. See various articles in *Il canto piano nell'era della stampa*, Atti del convegno internazionale di studi sul canto liturgico nei secoli XV–XVIII (1998), ed. Giulio Cattin, Danilo Curti, Marco Gozzi (Trent: Provincia autonoma, 1999); Thomas Forrest Kelly, ed., *Plainsong in the Age of Polyphony*, Cambridge Studies in Performance Practice 2 (Cambridge: Cambridge University Press, 1992); Marco Gozzi, "L'edizione veneziana del Graduale curata da Vecchi, Balbi e Gabrieli (1591)," *Polifonie* 5, no. 3 (2005): 9–22 (English translation: "The Venetian edition of the Gradual revised by Vecchi, Balbi and Gabrieli [1591]," 33–46); and Theodore Karp, *An Introduction to the Post-Tridentine Mass Proper*, 2 parts (Middleton, Wisc.: American Institute of Musicology, 2005).

3. Paola Besutti, *Un tardivo repertorio di canto piano*, in *Tradizione manoscritta e pratica musicale: I codici di Puglia*, Atti del convegno (Bari, October 30–31, 1986), ed. Dinko Fabris and Anselmo Susca, Quaderni della Rivista Italiana di Musicologia 23 (Florence: Olschki, 1990), 87–97; Besutti, "Testi e melodie per la cappella di Santa Barbara in Mantova," in *Trasmissione e recezione delle forme di cultura musicale*, vol. 2, *Study sessions*, Atti del XIV congresso della Società Internazionale di Musicologia (Bologna, August 27–September 1, 1987), ed. Lorenzo Bianconi, F. Alberto Gallo, Angelo Pompilio, and Donatella Restani (Turin: EDT, 1990), 68–77; Angelo Rusconi, "Il canto del rito 'patriarchino' nell'antica diocesi di Como: Ricerche preliminari sulla tradizione scritta," in *Il canto patriarchino di tradizione orale in area veneto-friulana e istriana*, Atti del seminario di studio (Venice, Fondazione Ugo e Olga Levi, May 8–10, 1997), ed. Paola Barzan and Anna Vildera, Cultura popolare veneta, n.s., 4 (Vicenza: Neri Pozza, 2000), 249–288; Rusconi, "Atlantide musicale: Il canto patriarchino fra mito e realtà," in *Frammenti di storia medievale: Stato delle ricerche sui manoscritti di canto liturgico*, Atti del convegno (Spoleto, October 2–3, 1999), ed. Gioia Filocamo, Historiae Musicae Cultores 91 (Florence: Olschki, 2002), 53–67.

4. Ernesto Teodoro Moneta Caglio, "I corali di S. Nazaro," in *La Basilica degli Apostoli e Nazaro Martire nel culto e nell'arte* (Milan: Cazzaniga, 1969).

The origin of this lack, perhaps, is the fairly common idea that the Milanese tradition was passed down homogeneously through the centuries, yielding sources that are rather similar to one another. Actually, a facsimile edition of only one Ambrosian musical manuscript is available today: the fifth volume of the Solesmes *Paléographie musicale*, issued in 1899, which contains only the winter part of a twelfth-century antiphonary of unknown origin and provenance. Also available now are the Houghton manuscripts, in digital form. A facsimile edition of the Vendrogno antiphonary will be published in *Paléographie musicale*. But the real situation is quite different. In many respects, a number of relevant variants are already present in medieval manuscripts. In Renaissance books we find other complicated problems.

Furthermore, in recent years, Ambrosian chant studies in Italy shared the same views as the older studies of Gregorian chant, with attempts to identify the "archaic" and "authentic" group of Milanese melodies: this brought about the publication of a new *Antiphonale missarum*, presented as the "true" Milanese antiphonary.[5] From this, it is clear that Ambrosian chant studies urgently requires new attention from individual scholars and institutions collaborating in well-conceived and executed research projects.

As for the "new" sources, I will specifically discuss a group of manuscripts from a single location: three from the sixteenth century, one from the seventeenth, one from the eighteenth, and four from the nineteenth—a total of nine manuscripts—as well as many separate fascicles. In discussing special problems, other late sources, known and previously unknown, as well as one important printed book, published in 1618, will also be considered. Undoubtedly a number of late sources remain unknown and uncataloged.

I discovered the first group of manuscripts in the archive of the Church of Santo Stefano in Mariano Comense—a small town about twenty-five kilometers from Milan, in the region of Brianza—following a short note in Michel Huglo's *Fonti e paleografia*: "Mariano Comense: alcuni manoscritti cartacei."[6] Here I found six large manuscripts and many smaller books and separate fascicles dating from the sixteenth to the twentieth centuries. There was another manuscript there, as well: an antiphonary from the fourteenth century, presented to Don Guerrino Amelli and brought by him to Montecassino and Florence and having later arrived at the

---

5. This book shares the same format as the old Schuster/Suñol books; at the beginning, there is a letter by the archbishop. Nonexpert readers might think that this is the new official edition, replacing the old one, but it is not. Many pieces are newly composed adaptations. For the problems in this book, see Baroffio's remarks: "Il nuovo *Antiphonale Missarum* di Milano," *Rivista Internazionale di Musica Sacra* 27 (2006): 193–194.

6. Michel Huglo, Luigi Agustoni, Eugène Cardine, and Ernesto Moneta Caglio, *Fonti e paleografia del canto ambrosiano*, Archivio Ambrosiano 7 (Milan, 1956), 229, no. 231.

Benedictine abbey of Cesena;[7] having apparently disappeared from the abbey's library, it has now been found and photographed.[8]

Manuscripts from the Sixteenth Century

MS A: ingressarium (i.e., *antiphonale missarum*, chants for the mass only), written in 1543 ("1543 notavit suis expensis"; fol. 1r, fig. 4.1). The owner's name was cut out, but luckily it appears on folio 2r: "est presbiteri Io(hannis) Iac(obi) Cast(old)i can(onici)" (the book is property of priest Giovanni Giacomo Castoldi, canon)—a priest actually identified as a canon of Santo Stefano.[9] The name appears again, on folio 149r: "Sum p(res)b(ite)ri Io(hannis) Iacobi Castoldi Can(onic)i." The book contains Milanese Gothic notation, written on four lines in the Guidonian system; a portion of a line is added above or below the staff as necessary.

MS B: vesperale (antiphonary for vespers), written in 1540, in the same hand as MS A and also including the name of priest Castoldi.[10] When non-Ambrosian pieces are included, such as *Salve regina*, square notation is used.

MS C: notturnale (antiphonary for matins and lauds), written in 1572, in the same hand, and including the name of priest Castoldi.[11]

A detailed study of all of these books is not possible here. I concentrate on the antiphonary for the mass (MS A) to provide an idea of the contents of, and problems concerning, late Milanese sources. The book has an unusual liturgical structure, summarized in table 4.1. It begins with a first section (section A, nos. 1 to 21) including some feasts (without their vigils), from Saint Martin (as in old Ambrosian books) to All Saints. The next section (section B, nos. 22 to 71) contains the temporale from Advent to Pentecost (written down after Corpus Christi); however, the saints of the Christmas period have been included, after the

---

7   Huglo et al., *Fonti e paleografia*, 229, no. 229.

8.   The manuscript having been untraceable at the time of the Houghton conference, here I provide only a brief description: it is a summer antiphonary written in a Milanese notation of the fourteenth century. It was certainly written for Santo Stefano in Mariano Comense; in the masses of the Major and the Minor Dedication is written, "Iste liber est sancti stephani de marliano," in the same red ink used for rubrics.

9.   Ivano Bettin, "La pieve di Mariano a fine Cinquecento," *Canturium* 9 (2006): 66–71.

10.   Fol. 1 "[ ] pbri Jo. Jacobi Cast[ ]"; fol. 142 "P(resbiter) Jo. Jacobus Castoldus 1540 notavit suis expensis"; fol. 147v "p(res)b(ite)r Jo. Jac(obu)s Cast(oldu)s."

11.   Fol. 150v: "P(res)b(ite)r Jo(hannes) Jac(obu)s Cast(oldu)s can(oni)cus hoc opus suis expensis fecit 1572."

FIGURE 4.1   Mariano Comense, Archivio Santo Stefano, MS A, fol. 1r

Milanese tradition. The formularies for the Common of Saints and "de tempore" are placed at the end (section C, nos. 72 to 77). The fourth section continues the sanctorale (section D, nos. 78 to 131) and includes the vigils of the most important saints already copied in the first section (Martin, Andrew, Ambrosius . . . Omnium Sanctorum; at no. 120, instead of "Vigilia s. Mariae in Nativitate," "in Assumptione" was probably intended, as it appears in no. 124) and masses for the other saints. This sanctorale not only completes the first but also sometimes proposes new formularies for some saints—for example, Saint George (nos. 6 and 87), Saint Stephen (nos. 31 and 137), Saint James (nos. 35 and 138), and John the Baptist (nos. 9 and 105, this second time with his vigil, no. 104). Finally, a temporale section (section E, nos. 132 to 151) also presents new formularies (for some Advent to Christmas masses, nos. 134 to 138) and completes the second section with materials for the period from Lent to Pentecost (nos. 139 to 143) and various votive masses (nos. 144 to 151).

Table 4.1. Formularies from MS A

Section A: Sanctorale, from St. Martin to Omnium Sanctorum

November

1. Martini
2. Andreae

December

3. Ordinat. s. Ambrosii

February

4. Purific. s. Mariae
5. Agathae

May

6. Georgii
7. Philippi et Jacobi
8. S. Crucis

June

9. Johann. Bapt.
10. Petri et Pauli

July

11. Visitat. BVM
12. Thomae ap.

August

13. Laurentii
14. Assumpt. s. Mariae
15. Bartholomei
16. Decoll. s. Johann. Bapt.

September

17. Nativ. BMV
18. Mauritii
19. Dedicat. s. Michaelis

October

20. Simonis et Judae, Fidelis

November

21. Omn. Sanctorum

Section B: Temporale (including Christmas saints)

22. Dom. I Adventus
23. Dom. II Adventus
24. Dom. III Adventus
25. Dom. IV Adventus
26. Dom. V Adventus
27. Dom. VI Adventus ad s. Mariam
28. Vigil. Nativitatis Domini
29. In nocte sancta ad missam
30. III missa de Nativitate
31. Stephani
32. Iohannis Ap. et Ev.
33. SS. Innocentium
34. Thomae Canterb. [rubric only]
35. Ordinat. s. Jacobi ap.
36. Dom. post Nativitatem
37. Octava Domini
38. Vigil. Epiphaniae
39. Epiphania
40. Dom. I post Epiph.
41. Dom. II post Epiph.
42. Dom. III post Epiph.
43. Dom. IV post Epiph.
44. Dom. V post Epiph.
45. Septuagesima
46. Sexagesima
47. Quinquagesima
48. Dom. in capite Quadrages.
49. Dom. I Quadr. [!] de Samaritana

50. Dom. II [!] de Habraham
51. Dom. III [!] de Caeco
52. Dom. IV [!] de Lazaro
53. In ramis olivarum
54. In caena Domini
55. In die Veneris sancto
56. In sabbato sancto
57. In die sancto Pasce resurrectionis
58. Feria II in albis
59. Feria III post Resurr.
60. Feria V in depos. s. Ambrosii
61. Dom. I in albis depos.
62. Dom. II post Pasch.
63. Dom. III post Pasch.
64. Dom. IV post Pasch.
65. Dom. V post Pasch.
66. Dom. post Ascension. [!]
67. In die Ascensionis
68. In Vigil. Pentec.
69. In die Pentecostes
70. Corpus Christi
71. Dedicat. Maioris Eccl.

Section C: Commune Temporis et Sanctorum

72. Nat. unius apost.
73. Nat. unius mart.
74. Nat. plur. mart.
75. Nat. unius conf.
76. Nat. virginum
77. Officium dominicale ad missam [various pieces]

Section D: Sanctorale (suppl.)

November

78. Vigil. s. Martini
79. Romani
80. Pres. BVM
81. Caeciliae
82. Clementis
83. Vigil. s. Andreae

December

84. Vigil. ordinat. s. Ambrosii
85. Concept. BMV

April

86. Galdini
87. Georgii
88. Marci

January

89. Thomae Aq. [?]
90. Sebastiani et Solutoris
91. Agnetis
92. Vincentii
93. Babilae et trium parv.
94. Convers. Pauli ap.
95. Julii

February

96. Severi

March

97. Annunt. BVM

May

98. Victoris
99. Transl. s. Nazarii
100. Transl. s. Victoris
101. Quirici

June

102. Vigil. Protasii et Gervasi
103. Protasii et Gervasi

104. Vigil. Johan. Bapt.
105. Johann. et Pauli

July

106. Vigil. Naboris et Felicis
107. Naboris et Felicis
108. Mariae Magd.
109. Apollinaris
110. Vigil. Nazarii et Celsi
111. Nazarii et Celsi
112. Marthae

August

113. Maccabeorum
114. Sisti
115. Transfig. DNJC
116. Donati
117. Vigil. s. Laurentii
118. Hippoliti
119. Sisinii, Alexandri et Simpliciani
120. Vigil. s. Mariae in nativitate [!]
121. Bernardi
122. Genesii
123. Alexandri
124. In vigil. Nativitatis: sicut in Assumptione

September

125. Cornelii et Cipriani
126. Euphemiae
127. Satiri

October

128. Lucae
129. Cosmae et Damiani

November

130. Vigil. Omn. Sanct.
131. Vitalis et Valeriae

Section E: Temporale (suppl.)

132. Dom. VI de Adv.
133. Feriae Quadr. (cantus)

Christmas

134. Vigilia Nativ. DNJC
135. Missa I in nocte
136. Missa III
137. Stephani
138. Jacobi

Lent to Pentecost

139. Cantus Quadrag.
140. Sabb. in Tradit. Symboli
141. Feria IV post Resurr.
142. Feria VI in albis
143. Sabb. post Pasch.
144. Feria II–VI, Sabbato pro Baptizatis

Votive Masses

145. S. Spiritus
146. Feria II pro peccatis
147. Feria III ad poscenda suffr.
148. Feria IV de sapientia
149. Feria V
150. Feria VI de cruce
151. Missa BV

Possibly, the author of this unusual, but not illogical, organization worked from different books—perhaps organized in the traditional Milanese way, with mass and office in the same book—to make a book that partly imitated the new printed missals, where temporale, sanctorale, vigils, and votive masses were clearly differentiated.

THE CHRISTMAS MASSES

For Christmas, the various sets of chants included in second and fifth sections reflect the complicated evolution of the Christmas masses in the Ambrosian liturgy (see table 4.2).[12] The two sets in the second section correspond to the "modern" night mass, with the ingressa *Laetare* (no. 29, "In nocte sancta ad missam," fols. 35v–37r) and the third mass *Lux fulgebit* (no. 30 "Tertia Missa de Nativitate," fols. 37–41).[13] The second mass (with ingressa *Puer natus*) is not present anywhere, even if rubrics like "Tertia Missa de Nativitate DNX" and "Missa tertia" imply that the existence of a second mass was known; the only trace of this is the incipit *Puer natus*, added by a second hand and referring to p. 48 (*recte* 47v), where the piece is the ingressa of the mass "In ordinatione s. Jacobi."

Table 4.2. Christmas Masses in Mariano Comense MS A

	Section B (nos. 29–30)		Section E (nos. 135–136)	
	Night Mass	3rd Mass	Night Mass	3rd Mass
Ingressa	*Laetare*	*Lux fulgebit*	*Lux fulgebit*	*Puer natus*
Psalmellus		*Tecum principium*		
Alleluia	*Domine Deus*	*Hodie in Betlehem*	*Puer natus*	*Hodie*
Ante evangelium		*Gloria in excelsis*		*Gloria in excelsis*
Post evangelium	*Gaudeamus omnes*	*Ecce annuntio*	*Per viscera*	*Ecce annuntio*
Offerenda	*Spiritus Domini*	*Ecce apertum*	*Beata et venerabilis*	*Ecce apertum*
Confractorium	*Quis est iste*	*Magnum et salutare*	*Iuravit*	*Magnum et salutare*
Transitorium	*Hic est salvator*	*Gaude et laetare*	*Magnum haereditatis*	*Gaude et laetare*

The two sets in the second temporale are mainly cues referring to pieces already copied in the first temporale. The third mass is *Lux fulgebit*, but with ingressa *Puer natus*; the night mass uses two pieces from the set *Hodie nobis* added in

---

12.   See Terence Bailey, "Christmas Masses in the Ambrosian Liturgy," in this volume.

13.   The same two sets in Mariano Comense, MS D from AD 1634 (see below).

the *Manuale Ambrosianum* (alleluia *Puer natus* and confractorium *Per viscera*, here as *antiphona post evangelium*).[14]

"PROPERIZATION" OF THE SANCTORAL MASSES

A major problem in MS A involves the contents of single masses, especially those for the saints. Frequently, there is no correspondence with either the modern missal edited by Cardinal Ferrari in 1902 (and the related Schuster/Suñol *Antiphonale Missarum*) or older manuscripts like Vimercate and others. The oldest and most modern books often have recurrent pieces for the saints. Here we find an attempt to offer "more proper" masses. This is achieved by using proper chants from the office in the mass: responsories *cum infantibus* or *in choro* became offertories; psallendae, antiphons *ad Magnificat*, and antiphons *in choro* became antiphons *post evangelium*, confractoria, and transitoria.

Sometimes, there is the "normal" mass and a new one. For example, two sets are offered for Saint Stephen. In the first temporale, the normal set is given, and even has a second offerenda copied at the end; the second temporale replaces the Christmas pieces, like the alleluia *Puer natus*, with pieces from the office and refers to a martyr and to Stephen specifically (see table 4.3). A third set is possible, because the first one has three "alia," and the second of them (*antiphona post evangelium Stephanum protomartyrem*) differs from the *post evangelium* of the second set too.

Table 4.3. Saint Stephen Masses in Mariano Comense MS A

	Section B (no. 31)	Section E (no. 137)
Ingressa	*Video*	*Video*
Psalmellus	*Stephanus plenus*	
Alleluia	*Puer natus* (rubric 2nd hand: *Posuisti*)	*Posuisti*
Post Evangelium	*Posuerunt* (alia: *Stephanum protomartyrem*)	*Posuerunt*
Offerenda	*Ecce apertum* (alia: *Coronam gloriae*, copied at the end)	*Coronam gloriae*
Confractorium	*Magnum et salutare*	*Tu principatum*
Transitorium	*Magnum haereditatis*	*Sepelierunt Stephanum*

In the manuscript, the "new" pieces are placed in second position as "aliud" or "alia": this contradicts the "loi des doublets" suggested by Gabriel Beyssac and

---

14.   See Bailey, "Christmas Masses in the Ambrosian Liturgy," in this volume.

articulated by Huglo for Gregorian manuscripts (with old pieces taking second place).[15] The same happens in the printed Ambrosian missal issued in 1522 (only twenty-one years earlier), where a similar situation obtains, although with many differences in specific chant assignments.

Two remarks are appropriate here. First, common pieces between mass and office were already present in the Ambrosian liturgy in the oldest sources. Second, the extensive application of such techniques to the sanctorale could be related to the increasing importance of saints in devotion and liturgy in the late Middle Ages. It also seems clear that before the Council of Trent even the printed missal did not impose definite and universal norms. Of course, this situation can be clarified only in the context of a comprehensive study of the history of the Ambrosian missal through the centuries, which is lacking today. Aside from the adaptation and reuse of preexisting material in the sanctorale, we must also account for newly composed masses and offices for new saints and feasts.[16]

CHANT OUTSIDE THE DUOMO

Manuscripts from provincial churches like Santo Stefano help show the practice of Ambrosian liturgy and music outside the Duomo. Generally, it seems that the oldest manuscripts are often the product or the reflection of centralized models (even if there are indicators that reveal whether a manuscript has been written for Milan or for a location in the countryside).[17] Often, the late ones more clearly show the particular use of the practice in a single church and, in general, of those churches not able to support a liturgy as complicated as that of the Duomo, which would require a number of specialized participants.

MS A, for example, does not include the psalmellus (the melismatic responsory sung after the first reading), except in the principal feast (here, the patron saint, Stephen) and in Lent. A similar scenario is found in the ingressarium in four volumes from San Vittore al Corpo (an Ambrosian Olivetan monastery at Milan), now at the Biblioteca Trivulziana.[18] Written in the same period as MS A, the Trivulziana manuscript does not include psalmelli in the single masses; instead, it adds them in a separate section, but recomposed syllabically (in Ambrosian style);

---

15. Michel Huglo, *Liturgia e musica sacra aquileiese*, in *Storia della cultura veneta* I: *Dalle origini al Trecento* (Venice: Neri Pozza, 1976), 314.

16. A particular case is the figure of Orrico Scaccabarozzi, who composed *historiae* for various feasts. The mass and office of Saint Galdinus have been edited by Amelia De Salvatore, *L'opera musicale e letteraria di Orrico Scaccabarozzi*, Benedettine S. Agata sui due Golfi (Naples, s.d.); the mass and office of Saint Uldericus, by Karleinz Schlager and Theodor Wohnhaas, "Ein Ulrichsoffizium aus Mailand," *Jahrbuch des Vereins für Augsburger Bistumsgeschichte* 16 (1982): 122–159.

17. Huglo et al., *Fonti e paleografia*, 4–5.

18. Milan, Biblioteca Trivulziana, A-1, B-2, C-3, D-4.

these often difficult and long responsories were transformed into simple, syllabic pieces.[19]

Psalmelli are also missing in nineteenth-century books, as in the two antiphonaries found in the archive of San Giovanni Evangelista at Lecco (with exceptions for Lent).[20] I do not know whether, at Santo Stefano and similar churches, psalmelli were not performed, were performed in simplified versions (as at San Vittore al Corpo), were simply read, or were given some other treatment.

From a musical point of view, examples show good preservation of the melodies in our manuscripts from the sixteenth and seventeenth centuries. By the end of that period, some neumes had disappeared, but the profiles of the melodies were still well preserved. By a certain time, however, manuscripts had been adapted to new needs and tastes. Before studying these adjustments, we must briefly describe the other sources from Mariano Comense.

MANUSCRIPTS FROM THE SEVENTEENTH THROUGH THE NINETEENTH CENTURIES

From the Seventeenth Century

MS D: a large Ambrosian antiphonary of uncertain provenance (from October's first Sunday to Maundy Thursday), written in 1634 (fol. 169r: "1634 p.a.b."—the meaning of the letters is unclear). Milanese Gothic notation, written on four lines in the Guidonian system. The manuscript is later than MSS A, B, and C, but it returns to the classical structure of Ambrosian books, mixing mass and office. It requires special study and probably reflects a considerably older source.

From the Ninteteenth Century

MS E: ingressarium, written in the first half of the nineteenth century. Square notation on four lines in the Guidonian system; as in other late manuscripts, isolated rhomboid notes seem sometimes to be related to unaccented syllables, thus having a different meaning than in traditional Ambrosian writing. Contains many additions.

MS F: Vesperale written in 1839. Same notation.

---

19. Angelo Rusconi, "Esempi di canti neo-ambrosiani," *Musica e storia* 14 (2006): 479–486.

20. I will call them Lecco, San Giovanni, MS A (by Don Carlo Gerosa, second half of nineteenth century, with old mark "O"), and Lecco, San Giovanni, MS B.

ADAPTING MELODIES

In MSS A, B, C, and D, the melodies have been adjusted in various ways: by erasing the original handwriting; by striking through sections with pen; and by inserting bars to isolate sections not to be sung. These corrections generally allow us to recognize, with precision, the original writing and compare it with the revised form.

In MS A (1543), corrections mostly appear in the psalmelli of Lent (the only surviving psalmelli, along with that for Saint Stephen) and in many other melismatic pieces. An interesting example is the offerenda *Precatus est Moyses*. In table 4.4, we examine, first, the originally written version, compared with the version proposed by the manuscripts Houghton Library MS Lat 388 (twelfth century) and Muggiasca (1388); second, the corrected version, as can be seen in MSS A (1543) and D (1634), from Mariano Comense; and third, a version found in a nineteenth-century manuscript.

Table 4.4. *Precatus est Moyses* in **Milanese Sources**

Only differences from the topmost reading are shown; /// indicates that text and music are not present.
In the table, h = B-natural ; b = B-flat.
Abbreviations:
HOUGHTON = Cambridge, Mass., Harvard University, Houghton Library, MS Lat 388, 12th cent., fol. 113r
MUGGIASCA = Vendrogno, S. Antonio, s.s., AD 1388, pp. 391–392
MARIANO A/1 = Mariano Comense, Santo Stefano, MS A, AD 1543, fols. 70–71 (original version)
MARIANO A/2 = the same (corrected version)
MARIANO B/1 = Mariano Comense, Santo Stefano, MS D, AD 1634, fols. 139v–140 (original version)
MARIANO B/2 = the same (corrected version)
LECCO A = Lecco, S. Giovanni Evangelista, MS A, 19th cent. 2nd half, fol. 13 ("modern" MSS version)

HOUGHTON	G	GahccGaG	FG	G	a		c	cha dedcha hchaG
MUGGIASCA								
MARIANO A/1		GahcGaG						
MARIANO A/2		GahcGaG						cha hchaG
MARIANO B/1								
MARIANO B/2								
LECCO A		GahcGGaGF	G		acha dedch		ab	aG
	PRE-	CA-	TUS	EST	MO-		Y-	SES

HOUGHTON	F	F	Ga	F	Ga	Gah	a	aG	F	Gah
MUGGIASCA										
MARIANO A/1										
MARIANO A/2										
MARIANO B/1										
MARIANO B/2						Gab				Ga
LECCO A		G	a	F	GaGab	a				Gaba
	IN	**CON-**	**SPEC-**	**TU**	**DO -**	**MI-**	**NI**	**DE-**	**I**	**SU-**

HOUGHTON	haG	D	DFFFD FGahG		G	////	////	////
MUGGIASCA	haGG		DFFD FGahG		a		ahccGaG	FG
MARIANO A/1			DFFD FGahG				ahcGaG	
MARIANO A/2			DFFD FGahG			////	////	////
MARIANO B/1			DFFD FGahG				ahcGaG	
MARIANO B/2	baG		DFFD FGahG			////	////	////
LECCO A	G	G	GahG			////	////	////
	I	**ET**	**DI-**		**XIT**	**PRE-**	**CA-**	**TUS**

HOUGHTON	////	////	////	////		////	////
MUGGIASCA	G	a	c	cha dedcha hchaG		G	a
MARIANO A/1							
MARIANO A/2	////	////	////	////		////	////
MARIANO B/1						F	F
MARIANO B/2	////	////	////	////		////	////
LECCO A	////	////	////	////		////	////
	EST	**MO-**	**Y-**	**SES**		**IN**	**CON-**

HOUGHTON	////	////	////	////	////	////	////	////	////
MUGGIASCA	F	F	Ga	Gah	a	aG	F	Gah	haG
MARIANO A/1									
MARIANO A/2	////	////	////	////	////	////	////	////	////
MARIANO B/1	Ga								
MARIANO B/2	////	////	////	////	////	////	////	////	////
LECCO A	////	////	////	////	////	////	////	////	////
	SPEC-	**TU**	**DO-**	**MI-**	**NI**	**DE-**	**I**	**SU-**	**I**

HOUGHTON	////	////		////	cd	c	Gc	hcha
MUGGIASCA	G	Gcc GaF acGF GF EFD FGacG		G				
MARIANO A/1		Gc GaF acGF GF EFD FGahG						
MARIANO A/2	////	////		////				
MARIANO B/1		Gc GaF acGF GF EFD FGahG						
MARIANO B/2	////	////		////				
LECCO A	////	////		////			Gchchab	a
	ET	**DI-**		**XIT**	**QUA-**	**RE**	**DO-**	**MI-**

HOUGHTON	ahaaG	FGa	GGccha ca GaFGahaG	GaG	GF	F	Ga
MUGGIASCA	ahaG			G			
MARIANO A/1	ahaG		GGccha GaFGahG	G			
MARIANO A/2			GGccha	G	G		
MARIANO B/1			Gcch ca GaFGahG	G			
MARIANO B/2	abaaG		Gca GabaGa	G	F		
LECCO A	aG		Gca GaG	F			G
	NE	**I-**	**RA-**	**SCE-**	**RIS**	**IN**	**PO-**

HOUGHTON	a	aha	GaGFG	G	FGaGcd	c	c	G
MUGGIASCA					FGaGccd			
MARIANO A/1					FGaGcdc			
MARIANO A/2					FGaGcdc			
MARIANO B/1								
MARIANO B/2		aba	GaGF					
LECCO A		aba	GaGF#				cG★	
	PU-	**LO**	**TU-**	**O**	**PAR-**	**CE**	**I-**	**RE**

HOUGHTON	Gachahch	a	Gah	aGhGaG FGahG	G	G
MUGGIASCA						
MARIANO A/1	Gachahc					
MARIANO A/2	Gachahc			aG FGahG		
MARIANO B/1				aGhGaGG FGahG		
MARIANO B/2			Gab	aGhGaG	GF	
LECCO A	GachaG		b	aGaaG FGahG		
	A-	**NI-**	**MI**	**TU-**	**I**	**ME-**

HOUGHTON	G	d	dedc	dfefgfed	d	cd	c	c
MUGGIASCA		G						
MARIANO A/1		d		dedcdfefgfed				
MARIANO A/2		d		dedcdfefgfed				
MARIANO B/1								
MARIANO B/2								
LECCO A	Gc★	cd	dedcdfefgfe	d				
	MEN-	**TO**	**A-**	**BRA-**	**HAM**	**I-**	**SA-**	**AC**
					LECCO A	**I-**	**-SAC**	

HOUGHTON	ccacdfed fed	ce	dccG	G	a	ach	hdeded	cd	c
MUGGIASCA	cacdfed fed		dcG				hdededcd	c	
MARIANO A/1	cacdfede fed	ed	ccG						
MARIANO A/2	cacdfed fed	ed	ccG						
MARIANO B/1	cacdfed fed	ed	cG				hdededcd	c	
MARIANO B/2	ca	ed	cGG				hdedcd	c	
LECCO A	cac fed	edcG★	G			ac★	chdedc	d	ch
	ET	**IA-**	**COB**	**QUI-**	**BUS**	**IU-**	**RA-**	**STI**	**DA-**

HOUGHTON	cha	c	c	aGF	G	G	a	GhahaGFFGF	aG
MUGGIASCA								GhahaGFEGF	
MARIANO A/1								GhahaGFEFE	
MARIANO A/2								GhahaGF	
MARIANO B/1								GhahhaGGFGF	aGG
MARIANO B/2								GbaG	aGG
LECCO A	a			aG	F	G		GbabGFEGF	
	RE	**TER-**	**RAM**	**FLU-**	**EN-**	**TEM**	**LAC**	**ET**	**MEL.**

This piece repeats the first phrase, "Precatus est Moyses in conspectu Domini Dei sui et dixit," with different musical elaboration. The repetition was erased in MS A. There are other small cuts, along with a large one in the last melisma of the verse.

In MS D (1634), the melody has the same cut at the beginning and is missing the verse *Et placatus* (fig. 4.2). Furthermore, some corrections have been made differently in the two manuscripts: see, for example, "animi tui," where, on the word "tui," the later version has lost the typical Ambrosian cadence G–a–h–G–G. Also, the second hand added a B–flat.

The last line of table 4.4 shows how *Precatus* appears in a nineteenth-century ingressarium for the Lenten Sundays from the Church of San Giovanni Evangelista

FIGURE 4.2   *Precatus est Moyses* in Mariano Comense, Archivio Santo Stefano, MS D, fols. 139v–140r

in Lecco. Cuts are quite similar, but stronger, here; melismatic passages are moved to accented syllables (see "Moyses," "Domini," etc.). Here, B-flat is original.

In the Gregorian version, the famous *Editio Medicea* (1614) cuts the repetition and widely abridges melismas (fig. 4.3). However, the Gregorian melody already places ornaments on stressed syllables. A better comparison for understanding such "corrections" is the Gregorian gradual *Omnes de Saba* as it appears in the famous twelfth-century manuscript Piacenza, Biblioteca Capitolare, MS 65, and its counterpart in the *Editio Medicea* of 1614.[21]

The most recent late-Ambrosian sources apparently revised the melodies according to the same guidelines we find in the *Medicea*. In sixteenth- to seventeenth-century manuscripts, revisions seem chiefly intended to abridge ornaments. In any case, the process of revision appears to have been slower and not centralized; the same chant is treated in different ways in different sources.

At the same time, we know from MS Lat 388 (fol. 113r) that the repeated phrase of *Precatus est Moyses* had already been cut in one of the oldest Ambrosian sources. This shows that cuts and adaptations are not always to be attributed to the actions of later reformers.[22]

Ultimately, the manuscripts show different degrees of changes. Sometimes, "corrections" seem inspired by principles similar to those involved in revising Gregorian chant in late Gregorian books. Some changes may have been due to musical and liturgical reforms in the sixteenth and seventeenth centuries. Others, as in Gregorian chant, seem already to have been present in certain parts of the tradition, even in earlier centuries. It is important to date precisely the changes made to the manuscripts and to carefully distinguish different types of, and reasons for, the corrections.

The research I have begun to conduct on late Milanese sources will cover many levels of analysis, clearly distinguishing different types of changes to texts and melodies. It will be possible to demonstrate changes due to such factors as evolving musical language, problems of tradition, changing tastes, and new cultural norms. The aim is to discover whether, at a certain time, there was a centralized revision of the Milanese repertoire or whether, on the contrary, every center worked by itself, reaching similar results within a common cultural and aesthetic milieu. At the moment, traces of both possibilities are found, but the second hypothesis seems more probable. One must keep in mind that Ambrosian chant lacked a printed

---

21. For a transcription from the former, see David Hiley, *Western Plainchant: A Handbook* (Oxford: Clarendon Press, 1993) 617.

22. See Baroffio, "La trasmissione delle melodie gregoriane." The comparison among Cistercian books and French contemporary sources shows that the "reformed" melodies of many chants already existed in local traditions. See Cristiano Veroli, "La revisione musicale bernardina e il graduale cistercense," *Analecta Cisterciensia* 47 (1991): 3–141, and 49 (1993): 147–256.

Dominica xij. poſt Pentecoſten . 231

Of-
fer-
to--
riũ.   Preca   tus eſt Moyſes in conſpectu

Do mini Dei ſu i, & dixit : Quare Domi-

ne iraſceris in populo tuo? Parce i   ræ

animæ tuæ : memento Abraham, I   ſaac,

& Iacob, quibus iura   ſti dare terrã fluen-

tẽ lac & mel : & placatus factus eſt Dominus
                              A a   j   de

FIGURE 4.3   *Precatus est Moyses* in the *Editio Medicea*, p. 231

edition before the end of the nineteenth century—only Suñol's editions of the 1930s had a relatively wide diffusion.

For the Renaissance period, a basic step of this research will be to compare the musical sources and rules found in such theoretical writings as Gaffurio's *Practica musicae* or the only extensive treatise on Ambrosian chant, Camillo Perego's *Theorica et pratica del canto fermo*, printed late in 1622 but written many decades earlier.[23]

The praxis of singing also needs to be studied (for example, the mensural performance of the hymns' melodies, supported by special notation in many sources, even if with melodies that are sometimes simplified). A number of them are found in a book printed in 1618 at the order of Archbishop Federico Borromeo[24] (see *Conditor alme siderum* in fig. 4.4). Figure 4.5 shows the only example of which I am aware of a measured version of the solemn Gloria; the source is a small eighteenth-century manuscript in a private collection. The Credo has the same notation.

Finally, this leads to a consideration of the diffusion of *cantus fractus* in the Milanese area. Apart from traditional melodies written with mensural notation, did new pieces reach Milanese choirs as well? At the moment, I have found only

FIGURE 4.4 Hymn *Conditor alme syderum* from Federico Borromeo's *Psalterium* (1618), p. 199

23. The original manuscript survives (Milan, Biblioteca Capitolo, II.F.2.24), and it is possible to compare the early and printed versions.

24. *Psalterium, Cantica, et Hymni Aliaque Divinis Officiis Ritu Ambrosiano Psallendis Communia Modulationibus opportunis notata Federici Cardinalis Archiep. iussu edita* (Mediolani apud hæredes Pacifici Pontii et Joannem Baptistam Piccaleum impressores archiepiscopales, MDCXVIII).

FIGURE 4.5   Milanese Gloria with mensural elements (Milan, Private
Collection)

some late examples in nineteenth-century sources, such as two Sanctus, which also present the organ *alternatim* practice (fig. 4.6, with only the sung sections notated). These are late sources, but an organ did play at Santo Stefano at Mariano Comense from the late fifteenth century.[25] Further, many Friars Minor were appointed as maestri di cappella and organ players in the churches of the region:[26] it is not impossible that they brought with them a music cultivated in Franciscan convents elsewhere.[27]

25. Studies by two scholars, Gian Luca Songia and Ivano Bettin, are forthcoming.

26. A panoramic view of the music in this region is now available in Angelo Rusconi, "La musica in Brianza," in *Enciclopedia della Brianza*, vol. 3 (Oggiono-Lecco: Cattaneo, 2008), 470–505.

27. *Il canto fratto: L'altro gregoriano*, Atti del convegno internazionale di studi (Parma-Arezzo, December 3–6, 2003), ed. Marco Gozzi and Francesco Luisi (Rome: Torre d'Orfeo, 2005); Il Canto Fratto: Un repertorio da conservare e da studiare, Atti dei convegni tenuti a Radda in Chianti dal 1999 al 2004, ed. Giacomo Baroffio and Michele Manganelli (Radda in Chianti: Corale S. Niccolò, 2005); Giulia Gabrielli, "Il canto fratto nei manoscritti della Fondazione Biblioteca S. Bernardino di Trento," Provincia autonoma di Trento–Patrimonio storico e artistico del Trentino 28 (Trent: Soprintendenza per i Beni librari e archivistici, 2005). Editions: *Cantoria: Pro Conventu S. Mariae Raddae FF. MM. RR. Scripta a p. F. Benigno a S. Joanne Vallis Arni superioris*, ed. Michele Manganelli (Panzano in Chianti: Feeria, 2000) (facsimile and modern edition of the Franciscan *cantus fractus* manuscript from Radda in Chianti [Siena], AD 1736, now in Trent, Biblioteca Lawrence Feininger, FC 131).

FIGURE 4.6   Cantus fractus and *alternatim* Sanctus from Mariano Comense,
Archivio Santo Stefano, MS E, unpaginated

The Notation of Ambrosian Chant
in the Eleventh Century

Thomas Forrest Kelly

W HEN DON AMBROGIO AMELLI, prior and archivist of Montecassino, brought to Montecassino a volume of Ambrosian chant in a calligraphic nineteenth-century hand (fig. 5.1), he was continuing a long tradition. References to Ambrosian chant, and research on what Ambrosian chant was like, had been going on there for a long time. It started with Saint Benedict himself, the founder of Montecassino, who used the word *Ambrosianum* in his Rule to refer to hymns.

Don Ambrogio had good reason for what he was doing; he had chosen the name Ambrogio, after all, and he was from Milan, the city of Saint Ambrose, where he had been sub-librarian of the Biblioteca Ambrosiana. It was he, it seems, who brought a bifolium from an Ambrosian antiphoner (fig. 5.2) to Montecassino (judging from its current folder, which is labeled "Framm. Amelli"; the fragment, by the way, is not listed in Baroffio's "Iter Liturgicum Ambrosianum").[1]

Amelli was a distinguished liturgical scholar. He published the remarkable poem, found in an eleventh-century Montecassino manuscript, that describes in verse a contest between the Roman and the Ambrosian chant, in which two boys competed in the singing of the two repertories, the Ambrosian singer ultimately being vanquished. (Amelli attributed this poem to Paul the Deacon, liturgist and biographer of Gregory the Great, and he assumed that the Ambrosian music described in the poem was that of Milan).[2]

Actually, neither Paul's authorship nor the identity of the Ambrosian chant in question can be established for sure. That is because there was another Ambrosian chant in southern Italy—the widely used local chant suppressed in the course of the eleventh and twelfth centuries. We now call it Beneventan chant—only because calling it Ambrosian would be hopelessly confusing—but we know that whenever people in southern Italy referred to their regional liturgy and its music, they used

---

1. Giacomo Baroffio, "Iter Liturgicum Ambrosianum: Inventario sommario di libri liturgici ambrosiani," *Aevum* 74 (2000): 583–603, available at http://spfm.unipv.it/baroffio/materiali/ IterLitAmbr.rtf.

2. Ambrogio M. Amelli, "L'epigramma di Paolo Diacono intorno al canto Gregoriano e Ambrosiano," *Memorie storiche forogiuliesi* 9 (1913): 153–175.

FIGURE 5.1 A nineteenth-century volume of Ambrosian chant:
Montecassino, Archivio della Badia, Corali s.n., 31 × 23

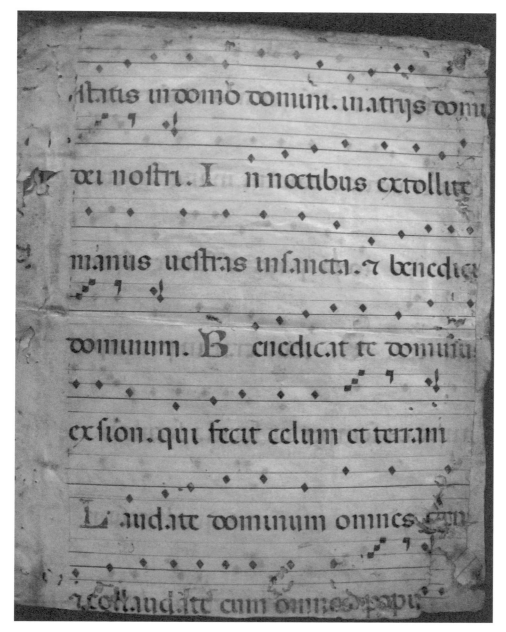

FIGURE 5.2   Montecassino, Archivio della Badia, Compactiones s.n.:
"Frammento Amelli," a leaf of Ambrosian chant, 29 × 23.5

the word *Ambrosian*. I have discussed this phenomenon elsewhere and listed the many references to "Ambrosian" chant in southern Italy.[3] The *southern* Ambrosian chant is the tradition that Pope Stephen IX famously wanted to suppress at Montecassino in 1058,[4] and it may be to this same local "Ambrosian" chant that Amelli's poem referred.

There are good reasons for calling the local music "Ambrosian": it is indeed related to the Ambrosian chant and liturgy of Milan, and both Terence Bailey and I have written about the connections between the Lombards of the north and those of the south.[5] The Lombard dukes of Benevento were at first appointed by the Lombard king at Pavia (not far from Milan); it is no surprise if the two areas shared a common liturgy. It is the geographical separation of the Lombards, north and south, and the fall of the Lombard kingdom to Charlemagne with the subsequent isolation of the south that can account for the differences—and the connections—between the Ambrosian and Beneventan chants as they survive in the earliest sources.

It is important, then, to bear in mind that the Ambrosian chant of Milan is related to the Beneventan chant of southern Italy, but that connection is only in the background here; instead, I should like to point out the presence in medieval southern Italy of the Ambrosian chant as we define it from the surviving Milanese books—the *Milanese* Ambrosian chant, we might say, rather than the local Beneventan variety. From now on I will use the word *Ambrosian* to refer to the Milanese chant exclusively and *Beneventan* to refer to the southern chant.

The musical history of the Ambrosian chant begins in earnest in the twelfth century, when the earliest surviving Ambrosian antiphoners—like Houghton Library MS Lat 388—were made. A few neumes have been added in later hands to earlier manuscripts, and a few pieces of Ambrosian chant appear earlier in manuscripts of

---

3. Thomas Forrest Kelly, "Beneventan and Milanese Chant," *Journal of the Royal Musical Association*, 112 (1987): 173–195; a list of "Ambrosian" references is given on p. 174. See also T. F. Kelly, *The Beneventan Chant* (Cambridge: Cambridge University Press, 1989), 181–182 (hereafter cited as *TBC*).

4. According to the Chronicle of Montecassino, "cantus Ambrosianus in ecclesia ista penitus interdixit." Hartmut Hoffmann, ed., *Chronica monasterii Casinensis* [*Die Chronik von Montecassino*], MGH Scriptores 34 (Hannover: Hahn, 1980), 353. See *TBC*, 181. On the Beneventan chant at Montecassino, see T. F. Kelly, "Montecassino and the Old-Beneventan Chant," *Early Music History* 5 (1985): 53–83; T. F. Kelly, "Abbot Desiderius and the Two Liturgical Chants of Montecassino," in *L'età dell'abate Desiderio*, vol. 3, 1, *Storia arte e cultura: Atti del IV Convegno di studi sul medioevo meridionale (Montecassino e Cassino 4–8 ottobre 1987)*, ed. Faustino Avagliano and Oronzo Pecere, Miscellanea cassinese 67 (Montecassino: Pubblicazioni cassinesi, 1992), 389–411; and *TBC*, 30–40.

5. Terence Bailey, "Ambrosian Chant in Southern Italy," *Journal of the Plainsong and Medieval Music Society* 6 (1983): 1–7; Kelly, "Beneventan and Milanese Chant"; *TBC*, 181–203.

northern Italy and southern Germany; these latter appear to be pieces adapted for use in the Roman liturgy and notated in whatever style was locally available.[6]

Ambrosian chants appear in southern Italy, however, from the early eleventh century, and it is that phenomenon that I should like to discuss here: we think we can understand why the singers of southern Italy were interested in Ambrosian chant, but we cannot be sure of how they managed to learn about it. Two new sources may help to clarify the issues.

We are well aware of twelfth-century sources of Ambrosian chant from southern Italy. I have pointed out elsewhere that the late twelfth-century antiphoner Benevento, Biblioteca Capitolare, MS 21, a manuscript of Gregorian chant, includes series of antiphons for Saint Apollinaris and for Saints Nazarius and Celsus that bear exactly the same melodies as are found in Ambrosian antiphoners.[7] Terence Bailey, in a paper that he generously shared with me before its publication, has discussed the famous Vatican flyleaf in the Ottoboni collection.[8] That fragment reproduces music from Tuesday through Thursday of the second week of Lent according to the Ambrosian rite; the leaf once belonged to Montecassino, and it looks to me to have been written there: perhaps it was a matter of research, of some twelfth-century Don Ambrogio Amelli wishing to find out whether the local *cantus ambrosianus* had any relationship to its Milanese counterpart.

For those sources, it is entirely possible that a notated manuscript of Ambrosian chant, even one that is still extant, served as the source of this music, for our earliest Ambrosian manuscripts come from around the same time. But now I should like to point out two examples of Ambrosian chant in southern Italy from about a century earlier, from a time, that is to say, well before the earliest known books of Ambrosian chant.

6. They include the antiphon *Dicant nunc Iudei*, three transitoria found in a few northern manuscripts, and the special pieces *Tenebrae* and *Vadis propitiator.* On the sources, see Michel Huglo, Luigi Agustoni, Eugène Cardine, and Ernesto Moneta Caglio, *Fonti e paleografia del canto ambrosiano,* Archivio Ambrosiano 7 (Milan, 1956), 10–32, nos. 22–49. See also René-Jean Hesbert, "Le répons 'Tenebrae' dans les liturgies Romaine, Milanaise et Bénéventaine. Contribution à l'histoire d'une interpolation évangélique," *Revue grégorienne* 19 (1934): 4–24, 57–65, 84–89; 20 (1935): 1–14, 201–213; 21 (1936): 44–62, 201 213; 22 (1937): 121–136; 23 (1938): 20–26, 41–54, 81–98, 140–143, 161–170; 24 (1939): 44–63, 121–139, 161–172. On the *Vadis propitiator*, see Hesbert's unsigned study in the introduction to *Paléographie musicale 14, Le Codex 10673 de la Bibliothèque Vaticane fonds latin (XIe siècle): Graduel Bénéventain* (1931; repr., Berne: Lang, 1971), 277–283.

7. Thomas Forrest Kelly, "Non-Gregorian Music in an Antiphoner of Benevento," *Journal of Musicology* 5 (1987): 478–497, esp. 488–184. A complete facsimile of the manuscript is *Paléographie musicale* 22 (Solesmes, 2001).

8. Vatican City, Biblioteca Apostolica Vaticana, Ottob. lat. 3. The flyleaf is reproduced in Henry Marriott Bannister, *Monumenti Vaticani di paleografia musicale latina* (Leipzig: Harassowitz, 1913), vol. 2, pl. 72; see also vol. 1, no. 354, p. 124. Another facsimile appears in *Paléographie musicale 14,* pll. XXXII–XXXIII. Bailey's paper has appeared as "A Lost Ambrosian Antiphoner of Southern Italy," *Plainsong and Medieval Music* 17 (2008): 1–22, including a facsimile.

The first of these is in an eleventh-century gradual from Benevento, the handsome MS 40 of the Biblioteca Capitolare of Benevento Cathedral. This book is famous as one of the principal sources of Beneventan chant and as a repository of a large local and international repertory of tropes and sequences.[9] Here, though, I want to focus on the feast of Saints Nazarius and Celsus, which is celebrated in Benevento 40 with a mass drawn from the Common of Saints;[10] after that mass, however, is presented another mass ("alia missa"), which begins with the Ambrosian ingressa *Reddidit iustis* (fig. 5.3). It is called an introit and fitted out with a psalm verse in the manner of the Roman liturgy, but it is the Ambrosian ingressa. From a comparison (fig. 5.4) it is clear that the Beneventan version is essentially that of Ambrosian chant, with a few filled-in thirds missing here and there. They are, I think we can agree, the same piece.

The musical notation, however, is different. The Beneventan scribe uses the traditions of his region and does not copy an Ambrosian version. Note that the Ambrosian lozenges are not present in the Beneventan version and that the classic Ambrosian way of writing series of descending notes (some examples are marked with arrows)—that is, by connecting the first two of them—is not observed by the Beneventan scribe. He writes in his own tradition: either this scribe is not copying from a written exemplar, or he is translating what he sees into the local style of notation.

We know that Beneventan script was subject to fairly rigid rules, and it appears that musical scribes too agreed to certain rules about how to write music.[11] We do not have any Ambrosian manuscripts from the early eleventh century, so we cannot be sure what a written exemplar would have looked like—but there seems little reason to doubt that some of the things that remain characteristic of Ambrosian musical writing were there from the beginning.

A *Gloria in excelsis* follows immediately after the Ambrosian ingressa in

---

9. The manuscript has been published in facsimile as *Benevento Biblioteca Capitolare 40 Graduale*, ed. Nino Albarosa and Alberto Turco (Codices gregoriani, 1; Padua: La Linea Editrice, 1991); for a description see Jean Mallet and André Thibaut, *Les manuscrits en écriture bénéventaine de la Bibliothèque capitulaire de Bénévent*, 3 vols. (vol. 1 Paris: CNRS, 1984; vols. 2–3 Paris: CNRS and Turnhout: Brepols, 1997), vol. 2, pp. 248–254, with bibliography; the liturgical contents are analyzed in vol. 3.

10. The mass begins on folio 102v: Int. *Clamaverunt*, Gr. *Clamaverunt*, All. de mart. Of. *Anima nostra*, Comm. *Justorum animae*.

11. The standard work on Beneventan writing is Elias Avery Lowe, *The Beneventan Script: A History of the South Italian Minuscule*. 2d ed., prepared and enlarged by Virginia Brown, 2 vols. (Sussidi eruditi 33–34; Rome: Storia e Letteratura, 1980; an expanded version of the 1st ed., Oxford: Clarendon 1914). The most comprehensive study of Beneventan musical notation is "Étude sur la notation bénéventaine" in *Paléographie musicale 15, Le Codex VI.34 de la Bibliothèque Capitulaire de Bénévent (XIe–XIIe): Graduel de Bénévent avec prosaire et tropaire* (1937; repr., Berne: Lang, 1971), 71–161.

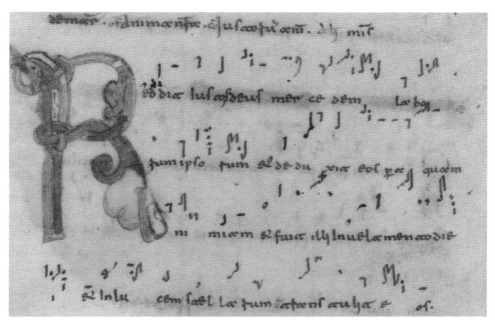

FIGURE 5.3   Benevento, Biblioteca Capitolare, MS 40, fol. 102v, detail: Ambrosian ingressa *Reddidit iustis*, 8 × 11.5

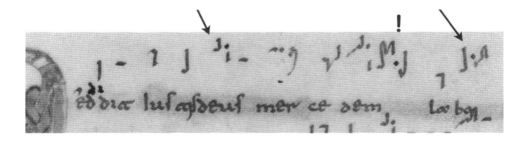

FIGURE 5.4   The ingressa *Reddidit iustis*, Benevento, Biblioteca Capitolare, MS 40, 2 × 9 (above) compared with Cambridge, Mass., Harvard University, Houghton Library, MS Lat 389, fol. 50v, 2 × 11.5 (below).

Benevento 40 (fig. 5.5); this Gloria is also Ambrosian and can be compared with the British Library manuscript published in the *Paléographie musicale*.[12] The rest of the proper items of the mass include two alleluias, a troped Sanctus, and cued gradual, offertory, and communion from the Common of Saints:[13] there is no further Ambrosian music.

A second witness of Ambrosian chant in eleventh-century southern Italy is found in another book in Beneventan script, this one in the Biblioteca Vallicelliana in Rome (fig. 5.6). This a composite volume containing a number of texts. The portion that concerns us extends from folios 138 to 173bis, written in the late twelfth or early thirteenth century. Its final fascicle, folios 167 to 173bis, is entirely palimpsest (see fig. 5.7). I have written about it before, and I was convinced then that the whole fascicle, along with a few folios from earlier in the manuscript, was

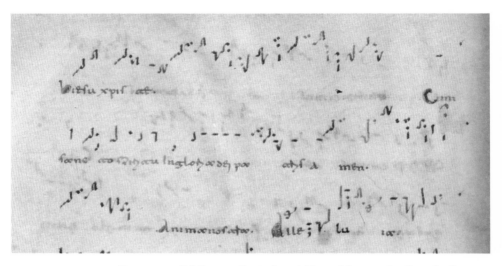

FIGURE 5.5   Benevento, Biblioteca Capitolare, MS 40, fol. 103r, detail: end of the Ambrosian *Gloria in excelsis*, 7.5 × 13

12.   London, British Library, Add. MS 34209; *Paléographie musicale* 5–6, *Antiphonarium Ambrosianum du Musée Britannique (XIIe siècle), Codex Additional 34209* (1896–1900; repr., Berne: Lang, 1971).

13.   Gr. *Anima nostra*; All. *Sancte Nazari*; All. *Sancti mei*; Of. *Anima nostra*; Comm. *Justorum animae*. For the Italian alleluia *Sancti mei*, see Karl-Heinz Schlager, *Thematischer Katalog der ältesten Alleluia-Melodien* (Munich: Ricke, 1965), no. 273, p. 196. The same mass is found in Benevento 38, folio 118v, but with two other alleluias, *Sancte Nazari vir dei* (Schlager no. 262, a Beneventan product) and *Te martyrum* (cued only: Schlager no. 397).

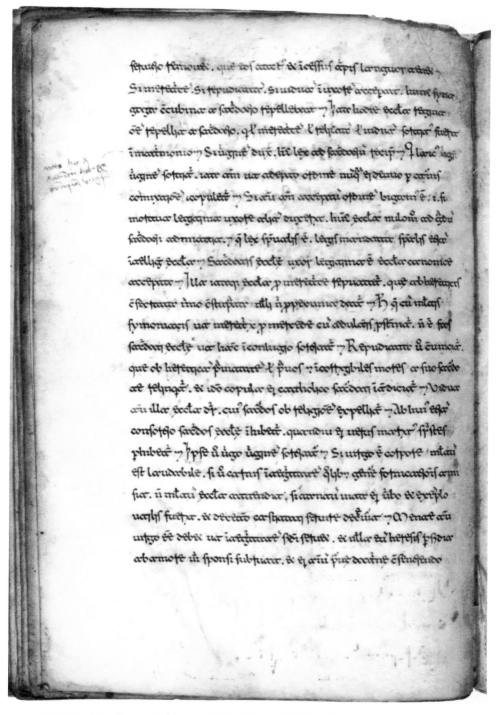

FIGURE 5.6   Rome, Biblioteca Vallicelliana, MS C 9, fol. 170v, 29 × 20.5

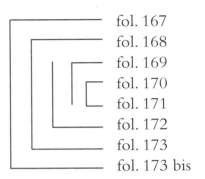

fol. 167
fol. 168
fol. 169
fol. 170
fol. 171
fol. 172
fol. 173
fol. 173 bis

FIGURE 5.7   Rome, Biblioteca Vallicelliana, MS C 9, structure of fols. 167–173bis

once part of a manuscript of old Beneventan chant.[14] That remains true, except for the central bifolium, folios 170–171. For the rest of the fascicle, at least some part of every folio or bifolio contains decipherable Beneventan chant.

The central bifolium, however, which can only be read on folio 170v, contains the end of the same Ambrosian Gloria just mentioned, and the Ambrosian psalmellus *Angelus Domini descendit ad Nazarium*—the next piece in the proper of the Ambrosian Mass of Saint Nazarius!

The reader will perhaps appreciate from the detail in figure 5.8 that I did not at first recognize what I was seeing. I did recognize the threefold Kyrie near the bottom of the page, and I noted that it followed the Gloria. And because all the other readable palimpsest pages of the manuscript contain Beneventan chant, I concluded that the Beneventan liturgy, like the Milanese, sang the Kyrie after the Gloria, not before. But I was wrong to conclude that, since what abuts this Gloria and Kyrie is not Beneventan but Ambrosian: unfortunately we cannot see what precedes the *Gloria*, but it is possible to see that what follows it is the Ambrosian psallenda *Angelus Domini*. Figure 5.9 is an image digitally manipulated by Professor Michael Scott Cuthbert, and figure 5.10 compares the psalmellus *Angelus Domini* in the Vallicelliana and a northern Ambrosian version. Figure 5.11 shows the end of the Gloria, as it appears in the Vallicelliana palimpsest, in Benevento 40, and in the British Library manuscript.

The central bifolium of this palimpsest gathering in the Vallicelliana may well contain only Ambrosian chant; certainly Ambrosian chant is the only music that can be deciphered. It is of course likely that the Gloria was preceded by the same ingressa for Saint Nazarius as is found in Benevento 40, but it is now impossible to tell.

14. Thomas Forrest Kelly, "Palimpsest Evidence of an Old-Beneventan Gradual," *Kirchenmusikalisches Jahrbuch* 67 (1983): 5–23.

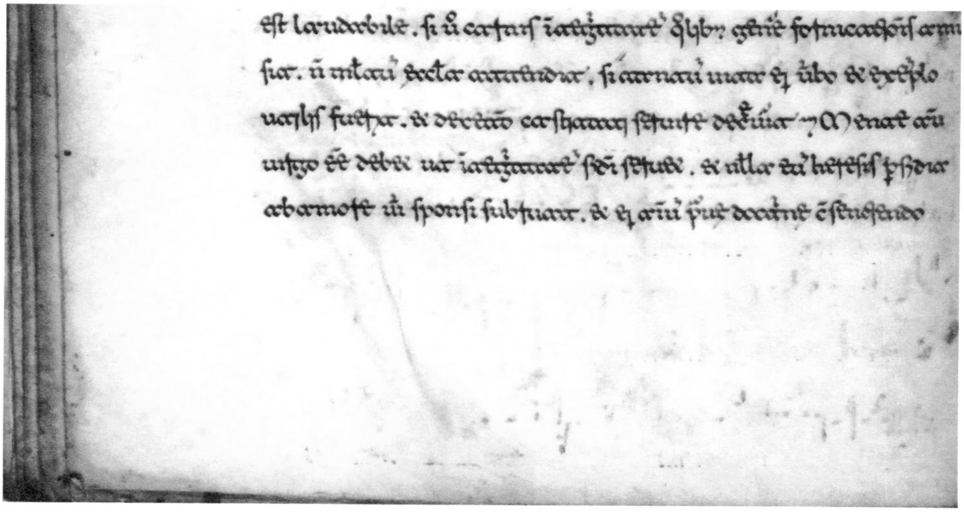

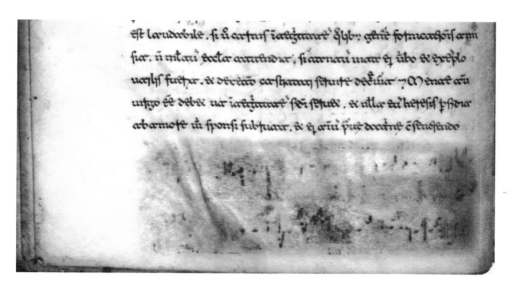

FIGURE 5.8   Rome, Biblioteca Vallicelliana, MS C 9, fol. 170v, detail, 7.5 × 19

FIGURE 5.9   Rome, Biblioteca Vallicelliana, MS C 9, fol. 170v, detail, digitally
manipulated, 7.5 × 19

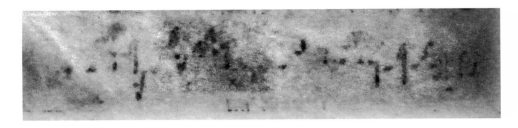

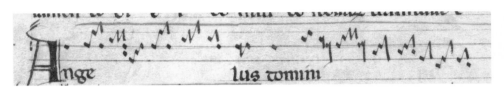

FIGURE 5.10   Details compared, Rome, Biblioteca Vallicelliana, MS C 9, fol. 170v, 2 × 13 (above), and Cambridge, Mass., Harvard University, Houghton Library, MS Lat 389, fol. 50v, 2 × 13 (below)

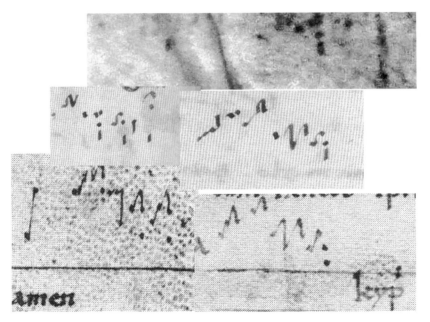

FIGURE 5.11   Three versions of an Ambrosian *Gloria*: Rome, Biblioteca Vallicelliana, MS C 9, 2 × 5 (above); Benevento, Biblioteca Capitolare, MS 40, 1.5 × 3 (middle); London, British Library, Add. MS 34209, fol. 131r (p. 261), reproduced from *Paléographie musicale*, 3 × 6 (below)

In Benevento 40 the Ambrosian ingressa for Nazarius and Celsus and the following Gloria were found in the context of a Gregorian gradual, adapted for use in a mass for the Franco-Roman liturgy. In this Vallicelliana manuscript, however, the Ambrosian chant is found in the context of Beneventan chant—and perhaps even in its correct liturgical place. Of the music decipherable in the palimpsest, the music on the preceding folios, though there are gaps, is in liturgical order, including music for Easter, the Exaltation of the Cross, Saint Michael, Ascension, Pentecost, John the Baptist, and Peter and Paul; the only music visible after Nazarius (July 28) comes two folios later, for Saint Andrew (November 30). Every folio or bifolium in the fascicle contains old Beneventan music, except for the central bifolium, the one that contains, so far as we can see, only Ambrosian music. It may be, then, that the Ambrosian music, at least the Gloria and the psalmellus *Angelus Domini*—and perhaps a whole mass—were borrowed into the Beneventan liturgy at some point before the making of this book. An alternate hypothesis is that the central bifolium happens to be inserted here but is in fact a separately circulating collection. The liturgical placement of the bifolium, however, and the similarity of script and layout, indicate that it is probably in its original place as part of a larger collection.

There are three points worth noting here, it seems to me:

1. The widespread presence in the south of Ambrosian music for Nazarius and Celsus;

2. The presence of Ambrosian music both in a Gregorian and a Beneventan context;

3. The eleventh-century transmission seems to have been accomplished with the use of musical notation.

For the first point, let us remember that Ambrosian music for Nazarius and Celsus is found in three southern manuscripts: Benevento 40 and the Vallicelliana palimpsest, from the eleventh century, and the antiphoner Benevento 21, from a century or more later (Benevento 21 is in fact the earliest surviving complete antiphoner from the area, so the antiphons might have been around for longer still).[15] Given that Nazarius and Celsus are Milanese saints, it seems appropriate that anyone seeking to create a mass proper, or to find some proper antiphons, should turn to Milan for source material. We do not need to posit an ancient Lombard connection or an awareness that Beneventan and Milanese chants are related to explain why southern Italians in the eleventh century might seek liturgical material from Milan for this feast.

---

15. The ingressa is also found in the later gradual Benevento 39, folios 132v–133r; the Gloria is not present.

The second point above complicates the picture, for if the Beneventan liturgy had originally included the ingressa and psalmellus of Nazarius (as it did in Vallicelliana C 9), and if the Beneventan liturgy was subsequently abandoned, even suppressed, in favor of the Franco-Roman, why would one piece of that older repertory be rescued? The scribe of Benevento 40, or whoever borrowed the ingressa of Saint Nazarius, may have been aware that it was not originally Beneventan and therefore not to be suppressed, or else he made his borrowing directly from Milanese sources.

The writing of the Ambrosian materials on the Vatican leaf seems to me to have been done by a Beneventan scribe, but in Ambrosian style. There are certain patterns—most especially that habit of linking the first two of a series of descending notes—that are entirely characteristic of Ambrosian notation but avoided in Beneventan.

Figure 5.12 compares the responsory *Angelus Domini vocavit Abraham* in the Vatican fragment and in MS Lat 388, from about the same time. Even though the Beneventan scribe uses the strong verticals and horizontals characteristic of the Montecassino *ductus*, the shapes of three-note descending figures is imitated from the Ambrosian manner. Arrows point out two examples in compound neumes at the opening of the piece, and as the piece continues there are some very clear "Ambrosian-style" climacus in the next line. It is a pity that the Ambrosian notation is so low that the text gets in the way.

It is important to know that Beneventan scribes (and Gregorian scribes almost everywhere else) as a rule do not make this connection of the first two descending notes,[16] so when we see the way the eleventh-century Beneventan scribes write Ambrosian melodies, we note the difference.

Figure 5.4, as we have seen, shows the opening of the ingressa *Reddidit* from Benevento 40, compared with its version in Houghton Library MS Lat 389. Arrows highlight places where the Beneventan and Ambrosian scribes have different practices for writing series of descending notes, the Beneventan scribe breaking after the first note. There is one place, however, marked in figure 5.4 by an exclamation point, where the Beneventan scribe has written a descent in Ambrosian fashion. This is perhaps owing to the fact that in his attempt to

---

16. See the study of Beneventan notation in *Paléographie musicale* 15, 132–133: "Nous ne pouvons guère citer, dans la tradition bénéventaine, qu'un manuscrit où le climacus de trois notes est écrit au moyen d'une clivis et d'un accent grave: [design of neume], comme dans les manuscrits ambrosiens" (here a footnote adds, "Il s'agit du n° 135★ [a reference to Ottob. lat. 3], qui, précisément, est un manuscrit de chant ambrosien, écrit en notation bénéventaine."The late Rupert Fischer, in an unpublished survey of the neumes of Benevento, Biblioteca Capitolare, MS 34, a twelfth-century gradual, could find only two cases of joining the first two of several descending notes, among the thousands of such descending configurations. I expect that a careful combing of Beneventan notations might well reveal a few more—especially in light of the presence of Ambrosian exemplars.

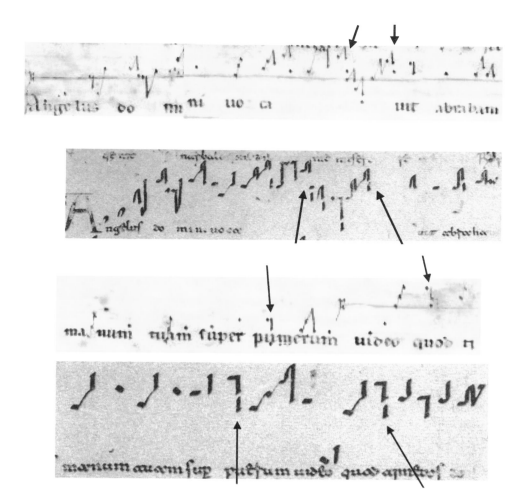

FIGURE 5.12   Portions of two versions of the Ambrosian responsory *Angelus Domini vocavit Abraham*: Cambridge, Mass., Harvard University, Houghton Library, MS Lat 388, fol. 115r, 2 × 10.5 / 2 × 4 (images above); Vatican City, Biblioteca Apostolica Vaticana, MS Ottob. lat. 3, fol. 1a recto, 2.5 × 10 / 2.5 × 8.5 (images below)

"Beneventanize" his transcription of a written document, he simply fails to make the appropriate adjustment.

Visible also in the Benevantan version, just before the exclamation point, is a quilisma. This sign is frequently found in early sources of Franco-Roman chant but usually disappears by the twelfth century; it is lacking in all source of Ambrosian chant known up until now. This version may suggest that the quilisma was a feature of the eleventh-century written tradition of Ambrosian chant.

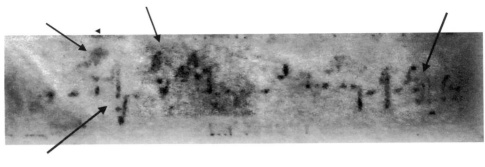

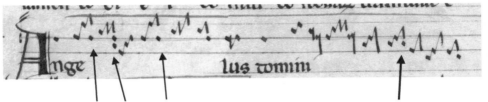

FIGURE 5.13   Comparison of two versions of the Ambrosian psalmellus *Angelus Domini descendit ad Nazariam*: Rome, Biblioteca Vallicelliana, MS C 9, fol. 170v, 2 × 13 (above); Cambridge, Mass., Harvard University, Houghton Library, MS Lat 389, fol. 50v, 2 × 13 (below)

The question really is whether the Ambrosian music was transmitted to southern Italy in written form or by some kind of oral means. I think it was written, and the palimpsest music in the Vallicelliana manuscript strengthens the case. The three places indicated over the second syllable in figure 5.13 are all instances of the Beneventan scribe's complying with Ambrosian practice in marking a descent by joining the first two notes. (There are occasional differences of melodic detail, but they do not affect this scribal practice.) The arrows on the right show one place where the Beneventan scribe uses his own practice of detaching after the first note.

There is no reason whatever that a Beneventan scribe would connect these pairs of descending notes on his own initiative. The suggestion must have come from elsewhere. These eleventh-century Beneventan scribes must have worked from written exemplars, and the exemplars must have been written using the conventions of Ambrosian chant as we have them in the later surviving Milanese sources. The southern scribes are more or less successful in translating the Ambrosian notation into their own style, and their lack of complete success gives us an indication of the nature of their sources.

We can also posit, then, that Ambrosian notation of the eleventh century employed the quilisma; for if the quilisma is any sort of ornamental neume at all (which we believe it is, even if we are not sure what the nature of the ornament is), then these Beneventan scribes have either heard the quilisma in the Ambrosian chant, or they have seen it. Given that we think their source was a written one, we must conclude that the written exemplar also included the quilisma.

These few sources, fragmentary and palimpsest as they are, give us an indication that Ambrosian music was written down, in essentially the melodic form in which it first appears in twelfth-century Milanese manuscripts, a hundred years earlier than the first surviving northern sources. The transmission of Ambrosian music to the south was accomplished in written form, but there is nothing to exclude singing as a part of that transmission. For all we know the Ambrosian chant could have been collected by Beneventans traveling to the north and either copying there or bringing back the written form—rather than, say, importing an Ambrosian antiphoner for reference. In any event, a written form of Ambrosian chant existed, and was consulted, at the time that the Vallicelliana palimpsest and the Benevento gradual were made.

It is not until the twelfth century, however, that there is evidence of whole books of Ambrosian chant in the south—the Vatican fragment, containing music for successive days, provides that evidence. The Mass for Saints Nazarius and Celsus, with its Gloria, may have been an isolated collection.

It is to the credit of unknown Beneventan cantors and scribes, who perhaps had the same pan-Lombard curiosity as Ambrogio Amelli eight centuries later, that we can now be confident that the melodic tradition—and the written tradition—of Ambrosian chant is at least a century older than the surviving northern documents.

Psalmody in the Ambrosian Rite:

Observations on Liturgy and Music

Michel Huglo

I<small>N</small> 1894 D<small>OM</small> P<small>AUL</small> C<small>AGIN</small> <small>WROTE</small> in his preface to the fifth volume of *Paléographie musicale* that by making the Ambrosian antiphoner British Library Add. MS 34209 available to archaeologist-musicologists, he was opening the door for them to a "catacomb" of the most distant antiquity. In fact, within the multiplicity of its liturgico-musical genres, the Ambrosian repertory preserved the two types of Psalter recitation of the early church, even from the period when the *koiné*, or widely used Greek vernacular, was still in use: first, direct psalmody (*in directum*), the recitation of the entire psalm without any refrain; and second, responsorial psalmody, the recitation of the entire psalm by a cantor with the interpolation between the verses of a short refrain sung first by the cantor and then repeated by the assembly.

Two Ambrosian antiphoners that were recently acquired by the Houghton Library at Harvard University are of somewhat later date than that of the British Library, but they are of great interest on account of their contents, because until now very few old Ambrosian antiphoners were known, especially with a summer volume. The importance of the twelfth- and thirteenth-century manuscripts of Ambrosian chant, such as those at Harvard, proceeds from the fact that they are the first witnesses to the melodies of Ambrosian chant, because Milan, like Rome, never notated its chant repertory with the neumatic signs invented in northern Europe in the ninth century. Before this time, then, oral tradition compensated for the absence of musical notation: the questions to ask are, for how long was this oral tradition maintained, and was it preserved intact?

To answer such questions, one must identify and compare the very oldest manuscripts with the texts of these chants with the later notated manuscripts, following the method Anton Baumstark presented in *Comparative Liturgy*.[1] Thus we begin with three psalter-hymnaries lacking notation but giving the texts of all ferial offices of the liturgical year, that is, the oldest layer of the Ambrosian liturgy: the Ambrosian psalter from Augsburg (Bayerische Staatsbibliothek Clm 343, from the

---

1. Anton Baumstark, *Comparative Liturgy*, trans. F. L. Cross, from the 3rd French ed. rev. by Bernard Botte (Westminster, Md.: Newman Press, 1958).

third quarter of the ninth century) and the two psalters in the Biblioteca Apostolica Vaticana, Vat. lat. 82 and Vat. lat. 83, which are somewhat more recent (described in appendix A).

These three psalters include the 150 psalms and canticles in Latin, following a version close to that of the Roman Psalter. A short collect comes after each psalm, conforming to a very old practice brought from the East about 415–430 by John Cassian, abbot of Saint Victor of Marseille:[2] Cassian informs us that the collect should be read after a moment of silent prayer at the end of each psalm. It is possible that these collects disappeared from use as the size of the office repertory increased.

The apocryphal Psalm 151 is followed by nine Old Testament canticles:[3] to these, two canticles from the Gospel of Luke were added, which are present in all Greek and Latin liturgical repertories: the Magnificat of vespers and Benedictus of lauds. In the Munich psalter they are followed by the hymn to the Holy Trinity, *Te Deum laudamus*.[4] Its Milanese melody with an E final is the same as the melody of the continental traditions, cited first in the *Musica enchiriadis* by Hoger of Werden, at the end of the ninth century.[5]

The Ambrosian *Gloria in excelsis* can also be dated from the early fifth century[6] since its interpolated verse—*Libera nos ab haereticis, ab Arianis, a barbaris*—no longer had any meaning after the great invasions, the sack of Rome by Alaric in 410, and the end of Arianism in the middle of the fifth century. The melody is sung in the same mode as the *Te Deum* (ex. 6.1).[7] Finally, after the hymnary on

---

2. The texts of Cassian, of the *Peregrinatio Aetheriae* (ca. 381–384), and of other authors are cited by Dom Louis Brou in *The Psalter Collects from V–VIth Century Sources (Three Series)*, Henry Bradshaw Society 83 (London: The Society, 1949), 10–16.

3. Heinrich Schneider, *Die altlateinischen biblischen Cantica*, Texte und Arbeiten 29–30 (Beuron: Kunstverlag, 1938), 99–126.

4. Maurice Frost, "*Te Deum laudamus*: The Milan Text," *Journal of Theological Studies* 43 (1942): 192–194 [edited from the three Ambrosian psalters]. The oldest witness to this hymn is the Antiphonary of Bangor (ca. 680–690), but with different final verses. Compare Frost, "Notes on the *Te Deum*: The Final Verses," *Journal of Theological Studies* 34 (1933): 250–256.

5. Hans Schmid, *Musica et Scolica enchiriadis una cum aliquibus tractatulis adiunctis*, Bayerische Akademie der Wissenschaften, Veröffentlichungen der Musikhistorischen Kommission 3 (Munich: Beck, 1981), 32–39 (cap. 11–14). On the author, see Dieter Torkewitz, *Das älteste Dokument zur Entstehung der abendländischen Mehrstimmigkeit*, Beihefte zum Archiv für Musikwissenschaft 44 (Stuttgart: Franz Steiner, 1999). There were frequent points of contact between Werden and Echternach, and Ireland and Scotland.

6. The Greek text of the "Angelic Hymn" is transcribed among the biblical canticles at the end of the *Codex Alexandrinus* (fifth century); the oldest witness to the Latin translation is again the Antiphonary of Bangor (fol. 33r).

7. In the manuscripts of the Ambrosian rite, the melody of the *Gloria in excelsis* is notated on three different scale degrees: Michel Huglo, Luigi Agustoni, Eugène Cardine, and Ernesto Moneta Caglio, *Fonti e paleografia del canto ambrosiano*, Archivio Ambrosiano 7 (Milan, 1956), 55, ex. 10.

folios 232r–236r, the Munich psalter transmits the Athanasian Creed, which was recited at prime on Sunday.

EXAMPLE 6.1

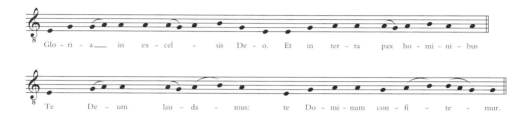

THE AMBROSIAN HYMNARY

The hymnary annexed to these three old psalters includes forty-eight hymns of eight strophes, each, except in the last four hymns, of four iambic dimeters. Of this number, fourteen were surely written by Saint Ambrose, according to Jacques Fontaine and Marie-Hélène Jullien.[8]

The notated hymns in the Ambrosian antiphoners and in more recent psalter-hymnaries can be divided into three groups by their finals:[9] twelve hymns on D, of which three are surely by Ambrose; six on E, of which three are by Ambrose; and twenty-six on G, of which eight are surely by Ambrose. In this last category, there is a hymn with a pentatonic melody, *Bellator armis inclytus*, for the feast of Saint Martin, on November 11, which opens the winter part of Ambrosian antiphoners.[10] A similar distribution of the three finals D, E, and G was observed by Rembert Weakland in his musical analysis of the office antiphons of the Ambrosian Psalter.[11]

---

8. See Jacques Fontaine, ed., *Ambroise de Milan, Hymnes*, Patrimoines: Christianisme (Paris: Éditions du Cerf, 1992); and Marie-Hélène Jullien, "Les sources de la tradition ancienne des quatorze hymnes attribuées à saint Ambroise de Milan," *Revue d'histoire des textes* 19 (1989): 57–189. Giacomo Baroffio, "La tradizione musicale degli Inni di Sant'Ambrogio," *Studia Ambrosiana: Ricerche e studi su Ambrogio e la sua epoca* 2 (2008): 251–261, counts only twelve authentic Ambrosian hymns.

9. Huglo et al., *Fonti e paleografia*, 98–105.

10. In the West, the feast on this day commemorates Martin's death; in Milan, it commemorates his ordination, which was celebrated on July 4 in the West.

11. Rembert Weakland, "The Office Antiphons in the Ambrosian Chant" (PhD diss., Columbia University, 2000), 448-449 (many on D and G, few on E).

THE MILANESE PSALTER

The organization of the psalms in the Milanese liturgical cursus must be considered not only as a mark of originality but also especially as an indication of its great antiquity: in fact, the 150 psalms are divided into three groups of fifty, as in the Gallican use of the time of Hilary of Poitiers (d. 367–368)[12] and as in Irish psalters.[13] But in the Milanese psalters and in two Saint Gall psalters,[14] the division into three groups of fifty psalms is not evident, because the decorated initials at Psalms 51 and 101 are of the same dimension and style as the initials of all of the other *deguriae* in the Psalter. This is also the case in some of the old manuscripts of Saint Augustine's commentary *Enarrationes in Psalmos*.[15] It is the liturgical distribution of the 150 psalms into three parts in practice that makes explicit the three groups of fifty.

The first group of fifty is divided among the three nocturns of Monday to Friday of the first week, and the second group of fifty among the three nocturns of Monday through Thursday of the next week. Finally, the third group of fifty psalms begins on Friday of the second week, so that the first psalm of Sunday vespers would not be that of the eleventh *deguria*, Psalm 111, but Psalm 109, exactly as in all of the cursus of the Eastern and Western Church. This remarkable break at Psalm 109 in the vespers psalmody owes its origin not to the practices of the temple but to the rhetorical selection of Christ's quotation of David, the poet of the Psalms, calling Christ his Lord (Mt 22:42–45).

In Milan, the office of vespers was preceded by the lucernarium, or benediction of light, according to a very old Eastern usage whose daily practice

---

12.   *Tribus vero quinquagesimis psalmorum liber continetur*. Hilarius episcopi Pictaviensis, *Tractatus super Psalmos, Instructio psalmorum* [i.e. *Proemium*], ed. Anton Zingerle, Corpus Scriptorum Ecclesiasticorum Latinorum 22 (Vienna: G. Freytag, 1891), 10. Compare Michel Huglo, "Hilarius von Poitiers," *Die Musik in Geschichte und Gegenwart* (Kassel: Bärenreiter, 2002), 8:1524–25.

13.   Henry Marriott Bannister, "Irish Psalters," *Journal of Theological Studies* 12 (1911): 180–184. Unlike the Milanese psalters, these psalters are not subdivided into *deguriae* of ten psalms.

14.   Saint Gall, Stiftsbibliothek, MSS 20 and 23. See Erich Kuder, "Illuminierte Psalter von den Anfängen bis um 800," in *The Illuminated Psalter: Studies in the Content, Purpose and Placement of its Images*, ed. F. O. Büttner (Turnhout: Brepols, 2005), 125 n. 82.

15.   Cassiodore mentions the "decadas undecim" of the *Enarrationes in psalmos* by Augustine (*In Psalmos praefatio*, in *Patrologiae cursus completus, Series Latina*, ed. J.-P. Migne [hereafter PL], 70:9B; *Magni Aurelii Cassiodori Expositio psalmorum*, ed. Marc Adriaen, Corpus Christianorum, Series Latina, 97 [Turnhout: Brepols, 1958], 3 [hereafter CCSL]). The following manuscripts contain the *Decades Aurelii Augustini super Psalterium* [Pss I–L]: Brussels, Bibliothèque Royale, MSS 5469 (Gembloux), 7980 (Tongerloo); *Quinquagesima secunda super Psalmos* [Pss LI–C]: Brussels, Bibliothèque royale, MSS 5563 (Gembloux), 7522 (Tongerloo); *Quinquagesima tertia super Psalterium* [Psalms CI–CL]: Brussels, Bibliothèque royale, MSS 5560 (Gembloux), 7981–82 (Tongerloo). Jerome mentions a division into five books (of thirty psalms each): that is the division of the Psalter of Saint-Denis (Bibliothèque nationale, MS lat. 103) and of Douai, Bibliothèque municipale, MS 70.

in Jerusalem is attested by the Spanish pilgrim Egeria about 381–384: she cites in this respect the *psalmi lucernarii*,[16] which probably designate Psalm 131, *Paravi lucernam*, and Psalm 140, *Dirigatur*, from which Milan and Toledo borrowed their responsories for the lucernarium. Also very early is the group of three alleluiatic psalms, 148–150 (*Laudate Dominum de caelis*), which were assigned to lauds in Milan as in the Byzantine church (the αἶνοι) and in the Old Irish liturgy.[17]

The forty antiphons appearing with the vespers psalms, the hymns, and other chants, which changed according to the feasts of the year, are written down in the antiphoners, but sometimes, only from the sixteenth century on, in a separate book, the *vesperale*—for example, that in the Free Library of Philadelphia for the use of the monks of Sant'Ambrogio Maggiore in Milan.[18]

This archaic distribution of the two groups of fifty psalms over the first five days of two successive weeks necessitated an exceptional organization for Saturdays and Sundays, and there the canticles of the Old Testament in the Ambrosian psalters found their place. Consequently, we observe that the psalms and canticles constitute the core of the Ambrosian office, to which hymns, responsories, readings, and prayers were added in a very complex order that varied according to the importance of the feasts.

THE ANTIPHONS OF THE MILANESE PSALTER

Turning now to the antiphons of the Psalter and first those with the first two groups of fifty psalms, we notice that only one antiphon was planned for the series of psalms of each nocturn, making a total of fifteen antiphons per week, times two, or thirty antiphons. At vespers, each psalm had its own antiphon, and thirty-five antiphons result, plus those for the Magnificat. Exceptional in this context is Psalm 90, *Qui habitat*, which was sung *in directum*, that is, without an antiphon, every day at vespers during Lent.

---

16. *Hora decima . . . dicuntur etiam psalmi lucernares sed et antiphonae . . .* Ezio Franceschini, Robert Weber, and Paul Geyer, eds., *Itineraria et alia geographica*, CCSL 175 (Turnhout: Brepols, 1965), 68 (*Itinerarium Egeriae* 24.4). On the antique Eastern hymn for the lucernarium discovered in 1878 by Cardinal Pitra in the manuscript Rome, Biblioteca Apostolica Vaticana, MS Vaticanus grecus 1070 (dated 1291), see Antonia Tripolitis, "ΦΩC ΙΛΑΡΟΝ: Ancient Hymn and Modern Enigma," *Vigiliae Christianae* 24 (1970): 189–196.

17. The fragment of an Irish antiphonary (Turin, Biblioteca Nazionale Universitaria, MS 882, N.8 (*ol.* F.IV.1, fragm. IX) includes the beginning of Psalm 148. See the rhymed collect following *Laudate Dominum de caelis* in the Antiphonary of Bangor (*Analecta hymnica medii aevi*, ed. Guido M. Dreves, Clemens Blume, and Henry M. Bannister [Leipzig, 1886–1922] 51:289).

18. Free Library of Philadelphia, Lewis Collection, MS 10, late fifteenth century. See Edwin Wolf II, *A Descriptive Catalogue of the John Frederick Lewis Collection of European Manuscripts in the Free Library of Philadelphia* (Philadelphia: The Library, 1937), 13–14. Eighteen other *vesperale* are cited by Giacomo Baroffio in "Iter Liturgicum Ambrosianum: Inventario sommario di libri liturgici ambrosiani," *Aevum* 74 (2000): 501–603.

At lauds one psalm was sung *in directum* without an antiphon, but Psalm 50 and Psalms 148–150, as well as the canticle Benedictus, were sung with antiphons, making a total of twenty-five antiphons. Thus with the antiphons of the psalms and canticles of Sunday, we obtain a group of approximately 100 antiphons that were repeated each week, even on the days of minor feasts.

These numerous antiphons from the Psalter, and those taken from the canticles, are extremely short, usually reduced to five or six words that were well chosen for their euchological value. They could be remembered as easily as their simple melodies, because at that time Latin was the *sermo vulgaris*—everyone's language. In reality, these short pieces are responsories, not antiphons—they were part of a system of responsorial psalmody attested everywhere in the East and the West from the fourth to the sixth centuries.

They were performed as follows: the *psalmista*, installed in his office by a priest, according to the *Statuta ecclesiae antiqua*,[19] began a short refrain, which was repeated immediately by the assembly (ex. 6.2). Then he intoned Psalm 83 (*Quam amabilia sunt tabernacula tua, Domine*) on the same pitch as the final of the *responsorium*. The medial cadence of this psalm verse in Milan and in Spain was reduced to a simple pause without any ornamentation. At the end of each psalm verse, the assembly repeated the refrain, *Cor meum et caro mea exultaverunt in Deum vivum*. This simple kind of psalmody was employed for the celebration of the divine office, as well as the mass, in particular in the chants that were interpolated between the readings of the fore-mass.

EXAMPLE 6.2

Saint Augustine often made allusion to this system: "In hoc psalmo quem cantatum audivimus, cui cantando respondimus" (In this psalm which we have just heard sung, to which we have begun to respond in singing).[20] In his different sermons, the bishop of Hippo commented on some twenty *responsoria* in use in

---

19. In the Eastern church as well as in the Gallican church. See Charles Munier, *Les Statuta ecclesiae antiqua* (Paris: Presses Universitaires de France, 1960), 98.

20. *Sancti Aurelii Augustini Enarrationes in Psalmos*, ed. J. Fraipont and Eligius Dekkers, CCSL 38 (Turnhout: Brepols, 1956), 529, Ps. XLVI, 1.

Africa at the beginning of the fifth century (see table 6.1). It remains now to determine how the *responsorium* evolved and was transformed.

Table 6.1. Responsoria from the Psalms Cited by Augustine[a]

Ps	Incipit
9:20	Exsurge Domine, non praevaleat homo
10:14	Tibi derelictus est pauper
18:5	In omnem terram exivit sonus eorum
31:11	Laetamini in Domino
32:1	Exultate justi in Domino
42:1	Judica me Deus, et discerne
49:3	Deus manifeste veniet*
50:11	Averte faciem tuam a peccatis meis
50:12	Cor mundum crea in me Deus
51:10	Speravi in misericordia Dei
61:2	Deo subjicietur anima mea
73:17	Aestatem et ver tu plasmasti
84:8	Ostende nobis Domine [misericordiam tuam]*
93:12	Beatus homo quem tu erudieris
100:1	Misericordiam et judicium cantabo tibi, Domine[b]
104:3	Laetetur cor quaerentium Dominum
115:15	Pretiosa in conspectu Domini [mors sanctorum ejus]
117:24	Haec est dies quam fecit Dominus*
118:96	Omnis consummationis vidi finem
140:2	Dirigatur, Domine, oratio mea*
140:5	Emendabit me justus
142:1	Exaudi me in tua justitia
145:2	Laudabo Dominum in vita mea

[a]Texts cited by Dom Jean Claire in *Études grégoriennes* 15 (1975): 179, drawing on the article "Afrique," *Dictionnaire d'archéologie chrétienne et de liturgie*, ed. Henri Leclercq, vol. 1, col. 630. The source is Saint Augustine's *Enarrationes in psalmos*. The asterisk designates R(esponsoria) in the Psalter of Saint Germain of Paris.

[b]*Misericordiam et judicium* (Ps 100:1) was sung in the home when Augustine's mother died: "Euodius took up the Psalter, and began to sing (the whole house answering him) [*cui respondebamus omnis domus*] the Psalm [*Misericordiam et judicium*] . . .." *Confessiones* 12, ed. William Watts, Loeb Classical Library 27 (Cambridge, Mass.: Harvard University Press, 1996), 58–59.

RESPONSORIAL PSALMODY AND ANTIPHONAL PSALMODY

The development of liturgical chant at the beginning of the fourth century is well known, thanks to the narrative of the events of the year 386 attributed to Paulinus the Deacon, the biographer of Saint Ambrose, and to Saint Augustine, in his *Confessions*: the Christians of Milan who were in the Portiana basilica under siege by the troops of Empress Justina, a supporter of Arianism, reflected their faith by the singing of hymns (composed on the spot by Ambrose) and of psalms, following the practice of the churches of the East, "secundum morem orientalium partium." This last phrase inspired commentaries by fourth-century historians of the church, which were collected and analyzed by Dom Cagin in *Paléographie musicale*.[21] It follows from this that the antiphony in use at Antioch in similar circumstances between 348 and 358, and later in Constantinople between 397 and 404, consisted of psalmody by two groups alternating psalm verses, no longer according to the improvised melody of the refrain as before in the West, but composing κατὰ τὸν τῶν ἀντιφώνων τρόπον, that is, following the mode of the antiphons: the term τρόπος in ancient Greek musical terminology preceded the adoption of the term ἦχος to designate a "mode" in ecclesiastical music.[22]

Moreover, in Jerusalem, the noble Spanish woman Egeria noticed, about 381 to 384, that the texts of the antiphons sung in the churches of the Holy City were no longer taken from the psalms but were adapted to the feast of the day and even to the exact location of the celebration, in particular, Palm Sunday.[23] An early non-psalmic Ambrosian antiphon is *Sub tuum praesidium*, the translation of an antiphon written on an Egyptian papyrus of the third century.[24]

It is certain that antiphony modified both the manner of singing the psalm and the function of the *responsorium*: from then on the psalm was sung by two choirs and the *responsorium* became the frame that determined the tone of the

21.   *Paléographie musicale 6, Antiphonarium Ambrosianum du Musée Britannique (XIIe siècle), Codex Additional 34209* (1900; repr., Berne: Lang, 1996), 17–23. Commentary by Michel Huglo in "Recherches sur la psalmodie alternée à deux choeurs," *Revue bénédictine* 116 (2006): 358–360.

22.   Sozomenus, *Histoire ecclésiastique* (8.8; *Patrologiae cursus completes, Series Graeca*, ed. J.-P. Migne, 67:1536B), as cited by Dom Paul Cagin in *Paléographie musicale 5, Antiphonarium Ambrosianum du Musée Britannique (XIIe siècle), Codex Additional 34209* (1896; repr., Berne: Lang, 1971), 17. The term ἦχος, a later form of ἠχή (cf. ἤχημα, ἠχήματα) was found in a papyrus of the sixth or seventh century, with mention of πλ γ´, πλ β´ and ἦχ Δ´, by Christian Troelsgård, who presented his findings in "A New Source for the Early Octoechos? Papyrus Vindobonensis G 19 934 and its Musical Implications," *Proceedings of the First International Conference of the ASBMH, 2007* (at www.asbmh.pitt.edu/).

23.   For example, the antiphon *Introeunte te, Domine*. See Michel Huglo, "Source hagiopolite d'une antienne hispanique pour le dimanche des Rameaux," *Hispania sacra* 5 (1952): 367–374, reprinted as article 19 in Michel Huglo, *Les anciens répertoires de plain-chant* (Aldershot: Ashgate, 2004).

24.   E. Mercenier, "L'antienne mariale la plus ancienne," *Le Muséon* 52 (1939): 229–233. The Greek text and the Latin translations are compared in *Paléographie musicale 5*, 74.

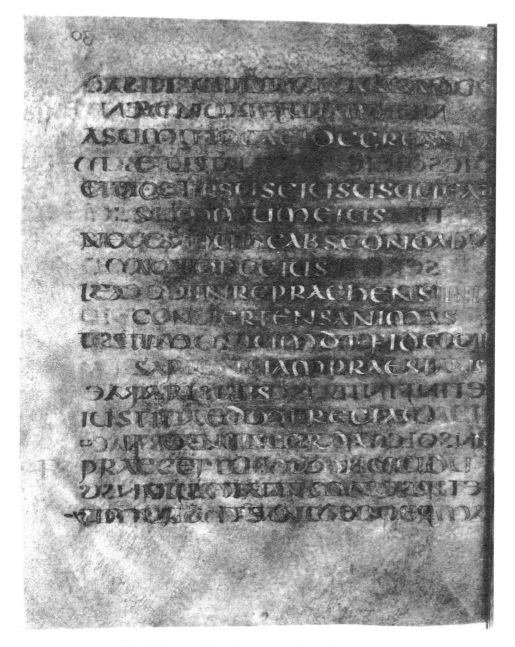

FIGURE 6.1   The Psalter of Saint Germain, Bishop of Paris: Paris,
Bibliothèque nationale de France, MS lat. 11947, fol. 30v, 27.2 × 17.5

psalmody. Nevertheless, the simple *responsorium* planned ahead of time for the chants of the mass would soon undergo a profound transformation, which we can assess thanks to two documents from northern Italy that are of the very greatest importance: the Psalter of Saint Germain, bishop of Paris, and a ritual of baptism from northern Italy published by Dom Césaire Lambot in 1931.

The Psalter of Saint Germain of Paris (d. 576), Bibliothèque nationale MS lat. 11947, was written, according to paleographer Elias Avery Lowe, in a center of high calligraphic standards, probably in Italy (fig. 6.1).[25] This magnificent psalter, written in silver uncial on parchment tinted purple,[26] has in the left margin of the psalm texts seventy letters *R* written in gold ink; in 1975 Dom Jean Claire, the first editor of these texts,[27] had considered that the Psalter of Saint Germain of Paris "could only be Gallican," contrary to the earlier opinion of Lowe. In table 6.2, one can read only the thirty *R*s that were reused as responsory-graduals of the mass (the *psalmellus* at Milan), or as a great responsory of the night office.

More revealing than the numerical order of the psalms was the classification of each chant following the liturgical order of the calendar (see table 6.3): the comparison between the Psalter of Saint Germain and the Milan antiphonary brought to light the surprising fact that one finds not a series of antiphons but rather a series of great responsories and *psalmelli* for the five Sundays of Lent, for the *Traditio symboli* (transmission of the Creed to the catechumens) on the Saturday before Palm Sunday, and finally for Holy Week.[28] There was a single exception, that of the fourth Sunday in Lent, when the *psalmellus* was taken not only from a psalm but also from the Gospel of Saint John—an innovation that deprives us of the

---

25. Elias Avery Lowe, *Codices latini antiquiores*, part 5, *France: Paris* (Oxford: Clarendon Press, 1950). In the facsimile of folio 171v, the R[esponsorium] just across from the second verse of Psalm 87 is barely visible. The marginal "R" indicates its location.

26. The use in antiquity of purple parchment for luxury manuscripts is witnessed by Jerome in his preface to the Book of Job (PL 28:1083A): his text was transcribed by the monks of Saint-Germain-des-Prés on folio Av of MS lat. 11947.

27. "Les répertoires liturgiques latins avant l'octoéchos: 1. L'office férial Romano-franc," *Études grégoriennes* 15 (1975): 179–180. In his edition, Dom Jean Claire resolved the *R* of the Psalter of St Germain with the word *responsa*, following Amédée Gastoué. The term cited by Dom Claire that was used in official correspondence in Rome (*Responsa sunt quae juris consulti respondere dicuntur*) must be set aside, as well as the term *responsio*, to return simply to *responsorium*. In my edition (*Schweizer Jahrbuch für Musikwissenschaft*, n.F., 2 [1982]: 59–60), I could find the letters *R* that were effaced or lost in the internal margin from the tight binding, thanks to the handwritten copy of the manuscript made by Dom Jacques du Breul in 1560 (Bibliothèque nationale MS lat. 13163).

28. This organization of the *psalmelli* of the Sundays of Lent probably coincided with the adoption of Roman tracts taken from the gradual psalms (Pss 119–133) that were chanted *in directum*. According to Dom Jean Claire, "Saint Ambroise et le changement de style de la psalmodie," *Études grégoriennes* 34 (2006–2007), the expansion of the Milanese Lenten period from three to six weeks was due to Saint Ambroise.

Table 6.2. R(esponsoria) from the Psalter of Saint Germain of Paris

Fol.	Ps	R(esponsorium)	Add. 34209
22v	16:8	R Custodi me Domine ut pupillam oculi	228 R/
59r	33:12	R Venite filii, audite me: timorem Domini docebo vos	220 R/
62r	34:13	R Ego autem cum mihi molesti essent induebam me cilicium	226 RP/RG
63r	34:23	R Exsurge Domine et intende judicium meum	257 RP
78r	40:5	R Ego dixi: Domin[e] miserere mei	193 RP
86r	44:3	R Speciosus forma prae filiis hominum	76 RP
87r	44:11	R Audi filia et vide et inclina aurem tuam	124 PS
87v	44:15	R Adferentur regi virgines postea	125 RP
90r	46:7	R Psallite Deo nostro, psallite	202 RP
94v	49:3	R Deus manifeste veniet, Deus noster non silebitur	1 RP
95r	49:7	R Audi populus meus et loquar	142 R/
95v	49:14	R Immola Deo sacrificium laudis	257 RP
97v	50:9	R Asparges [sic] me hysopo et mundabor	(174 A)?
98r	50:14	R Redde mihi laetitiam salutaris tui	167 RP
101v	53:3	R Deus in nomine tuo salvum me fac	151 R/
106r	55:9	R Deus vita(m) mea(m) nuntiavi tibi	180 RP/RG
117r	63:2	R Exaudi Deus orationem meam dum tribulor	221 R/
138r	71:18	R Benedictus Dominus Deus Israel	99 RP/RG
140v	72:24	R Tenuisti manum dexteram meam	RG
159v	79:4	R Deus virtutum converte nos	202 RP
160r	79:8	R Domine Deus virtutum converte nos	[129 R/]
162r	80:9	R Audi populus meus et loquar	142 R/
171v	87:2	R Domine Deus salutis meae	205 R/
183v	91:2	R Bonum est confiteri Domino	164* A
225r	109:3	R Tecum principium in die virtutis suae	60 RP/RG
225v	109:4	R Juravit Dominus nec penitebit eum	RG
235r	117:24	R Haec dies quam fecit Dominus	[Muggiasca[1]] RP
260v	129:1	R De profundis clamavi ad te Domine	156 183 R/
263v	131:17	R Paravi lucernam Christo meo	47 RL
276v	140:2	R Dirigatur oratio mea sicut incensum in conspectu tuo	162 RL

Source: Michel Huglo, *Schweizerische Jahrbuch für Musikwissenschaft*, n.F., 2 (1982): 59–60.

Abbreviations: A, antiphon; PS, psallenda; R/, prolix responsory; RP, psalmellus; RG, *responsorium-graduale* [Old Roman/Gregorian]; RL, lucernarium.

[1]See p. 111, note c.

incipit of the psalmic *psalmellus* set aside for this Sunday in early Christianity. In spite of this lacuna, it is evident that the series of psalmic chants for Lent in Milan, here made visible, is closely linked to preparation for baptism, administered during the Easter vigil.

Table 6.3. **Concordance between the Ambrosian Antiphonary and the Psalter of Saint Germain**

Date	Incipit	Add. 34209	StG	Lat 388
	ADVENT AND CHRISTMAS			
1st Sunday of Advent	RP Deus manifeste veniet v/ Deus deorum [Ps 49]	1r (p. 1)	94v	16v
Sat before Xmas	RL Paravi lucernam v/ Memento Domine [Ps 131]	24r (p. 47)	263v	46v
Christmas Day	RP Tecum principium v/ Dixit Dominus [Ps 109]	30v (p. 60)	225r	55r
St. John (Dec 27)	RP Speciosus forma v/ Eructavit cor meum [Ps 44]	38v (p. 76)	86r	64r
Vigil Epiph. (Jan 5)	RP Benedictus Dominus. Deus Israel v/ Deus judicium tuum [Ps 71]	50r (p. 99)	138r	78r
St. Agnes (Jan 25)	PS Audi filia et vide [Ps 44]	62v★ (p. 124)	87r	lacuna
St. Agnes	R/ *post hymnum* Audi filia et vide v/ Quia concupivit rex [Ps 44]	62v★ (p. 124)	87r	91r★
St. Agnes	RP Afferentur regi virgines	63r (p. 125)	87v	91v★

Sunday Quinquag.	R/ *in choro* Audi populus meus v/ Intelligite haec [Ps 49]	71v (p. 142)	95r	100r
LENT				
Each Monday	R/ *post Hymn.* Deus in nomine v/ Quoniam alieni [Ps 53]	76r★ (p. 151) *etc.*	101v	104r★
Each Monday	GR/ *ad matut.* Custodi me Domine v/ Exaudi Domine [Ps 16]	77v (p. 154) *etc.*	22v	105v
Each Wednesday	GR/ *ad matut.* De profundis clamavi v/ Fiant aures tuae [Ps 129]	78v (p. 156) *etc.*	260v	106v
Each Friday	RL Dirigatur oratio mea v/ Domine clamavi [Ps 140]	81v (p. 162) *etc.*	276v	109r
Each Saturday *ad vesp.*	A/ Bonum est confiteri v/ Et psallere [Ps 91]	83r★ (p. 165) *etc.*	183r	111r★
1st Sunday *ad missam*	RP Redde mihi laetitiam v/ Miserere mei Deus [Ps 50]	84r (p. 167)	98r	112r
2nd Sunday	RP Deus vitam meam v/ Miserere mihi Deus quoniam [Ps 55]	90v (p. 180)	106r	118v
ad vesp.	R/ *in choro* De profundis clamavi v/ Fiant aures tuae [Ps 129]	92r (p. 183)	260v	120r
3rd Sun *ad missam* [*de Caeco*]	RP Ego dixi: Domine Miserere v/ Beatus qui intelligit [Ps 40]	97r (p. 193)	78r	125r

Friday *ad vesp.*	RP¹ Deus virtutum converte nos v/ Qui regis Israel [Ps 79]	101v (p. 202)	159v	130r
Friday *ad vesp.*	RP² Psallite Deo nostro, psallite v/ Omnes gentes [Ps.46]	101v (p. 202)	90r	130r
4th Sun [*de Lazaro*]	R/ *cum pueris* Domine Deus salutis v/ Factus sum sicut [Ps 87]	103r (p. 205)	171v	131v
ad missam	RP Occurrerunt Maria et Martha v/ Videns Jesus [Jo 11:20–44]	104r (p. 207)	see p. 106, 108 here	132r[a]
Sat. *In traditione Symboli*	R/ *cum infantibus* Venite filii audite me v/ Benedicam Dominum [Ps 33:2] v²/ In Domino laudabitur [Ps 33:3] v³/ Gloria Patri & Filio	110v (p. 220)	59r	
Palm Sunday	R/2 Exaudi Deus orationem [Ps 63] v/ Discerne causam [Ps 42]	111r (p. 221)	117r	
Palm Sunday Ad missam	RP Ego autem cum mihi molesti v/ Judica Domine nocentes [Ps 34]	113v (p. 226)	62r	
Palm Sunday *Ad vesp.*	R/ *in Bapt.* Custodi me Domine v/ Exaudi Domine just, [Ps 16]	114v (p. 228)	22v	
Tues., Holy Week	R/ *ad Mat.* Exaudiat te Dominus v/ Mittat tibi [Ps 19]	116v (p. 232)	31v	

Holy Saturday	RP Exsurge Domine et intende v/ Non insultent [Ps 34]	129r (p. 257)	63r	
Holy Staturday Ad III[am]	RP Immola Deo sacrificium laudis v/ Deus deorum [Ps 49]	129r (p. 257)	95r	
PASCHALTIDE[b]				
Easter Sunday	RP Haec dies quam fecit Dominus v/ Confitemini Domino [Ps 117]	5r[c]	235r	

Abbreviations: A, antiphon; PS, psallenda; R, prolix responsory; RP, psalmellus; RG, *responsorium-graduale* [Old Roman/Gregorian]; RL, lucernarium.

[a]MS Lat 388 damaged after this point.

[b]The R(esponsorium)—"Alleluia"—is implicitly included in the title of the *Psalmi alleluiatici*: Ps 104, 105, 106; 110, 111, 112, 113, 114, 115, 116, 117, 118; 134, 135; 145, 146, 147, and 148–150 (sung each day *ad laudes*).

[c]Because London, British Libary, Add. MS 34209 is a winter portion, it does not include the pieces in this row. Thus the folio on which the piece appears in Vendrogno, San Lorenzo, MS s.s. ("Antiphoner of Muggiasca") is indicated instead.

The second document, a ritual of baptism from a north Italian church, in which the responsorial psalm is reduced to a single verse, contains a series of scrutinies for preparing the catechumens for baptism on Holy Saturday.[29] These scrutinies incorporate a small number of readings, each separated by a gradual or a tract notated with Italian neumes (see table 6.4). The ritual also gives three antiphons with verses. The last, *Venite filii* (Ps 33:12), is destined, as in other Latin rites, for the *Traditio symboli*.

---

29. Dom Césaire Lambot, ed., *North Italian Services of the Eleventh Century: Recueil d'ordines du XIe siècle provenant de la Haute-Italie (Milan, Biblioteca Ambrosiana, Ms. T.27.sup.)*, Henry Bradshaw Society 67 (London: The Society, 1931). Facsimile of folio 12r in Michel Huglo, "Liturgia e Musica sacra Aquileiese," reprinted as article 6 in *Les anciens répertoires de plain-chant* (Aldershot: Ashgate, 2004), facing p. 321. The neumatic notation suggests the region of Ravenna (by comparison with the neumes in the missal of Sant'Ambrogio of Ranchio, Baltimore, Walters Art Museum, W. 11; facsimile in Anselm Strittmatter, "Notes on an Eleventh-Century Missal," *Traditio* 6 [1948]: 328–340) rather than Aquileia, where German neumes were used.

Table 6.4. Responsoria from a Ritual of Baptism in North Italy

Folio	Category/Incipit
fol. 7v–8r and 25r*	GR Deus in adjutorium meum [Ps 69:2] v/ Confundantur et revereantur [Ps 69:2]
fol. 10v	GR Benedictus Dominus Deus meus [Ps 143:1] v/ Deus canticum novum cantabo [Ps 143:9]
fol. 12r	GR Ego autem velut surdus [Ps 37:14] v/ Domine ne in ira tua [Ps 37:2]
fol. 14r	GR Audi populus meus et loquar [Ps 49:7] v/ Deus deorum Dominus locutus est [Ps 49:2]
fol. 14v	TR Laudate Dominum omnes gentes (Ps 116:1)
fol. 17v	GR Auditui meo dabis gaudium [Ps 50:10] v/ Miserere mei Deus [Ps 50:2]
fol. 18r	GR Audi populus meus et loquar, Israhel [Ps 80:9] Hic non decantet versum.
fol. 18v	A/ Attendite populus meus legem meam [Ps 77:1] v/ Apperiam in parabolis [Ps 77:2]
fol. 19r	A/ Interroga patrem tuum et annuntiabit tibi [Dt 32:7] v/ Adtende caelum et loquar [Cant. Dt 32:1]
fol. 19r	A/ Venite filii audite me, timorem Domini [Ps 33:12] v/ Benedicam Dominum in omni tempore [Ps 33:2] v/ In Domino laudabitur anima mea (bis) [Ps 33:3]

Source: Dom Césaire Lambot, from Milan, Biblioteca Ambrosiana, MS T.27.sup (see note 29).

Abbreviations: A/, antiphon; GR, graduale; TR, tractus; v/ versus.

The interest of these two manuscripts, the north Italian Psalter of Saint Germain of Paris and the north Italian ritual for baptism, is that they present two situations parallel to that of Milan, in two important churches of northern Italy. The former manuscript, written on purple parchment, could indeed come from Monza, the capital of the Lombard kings, who must have adopted the Roman liturgy in the Carolingian period. The second document, the ritual of baptism, seems to have originated in the region of Ravenna, to judge from its neumatic notation.

Thus the two Italian manuscripts confirm the assertion of Isidore of Seville (d. 636) that the responsories were invented much earlier by the Italians, and that the Greeks had been the first to compose the antiphons chanted in alternation by two choirs, a manner of performance imitated by Ambrose and thereafter throughout the West.[30]

Four rules, apparent from a study of these two north Italian manuscripts, determined the choice of the texts of the *psalmelli*, the great responsories, and the responsory-graduals in the leading churches of Christianity in the fourth and fifth centuries:

1. When a passage of a psalm is chosen for a *responsorium*, the incipit of this psalm must reappear in the verse of the responsory.

    This rule, which follows naturally from the mode of performance of the responsorial psalm, is observed in thirty-four Old Roman and Gregorian graduals. In Milan, I found only two exceptions to this initial rule. One is the responsory *Domine Deus virtutum*, for the feast of Saint Severus of Ravenna, celebrated on the first day of February, evidently a late composition. The second exception is the second responsory of Palm Sunday, *Exaudi Deus* (see table 6.3).

2. When the incipit of a psalm is chosen as a responsory, the verse of this responsory must be taken from the same psalm.

    The first two rules were forgotten later on when other books of the Bible were used for the composition of the responsories of matins, notably those of Advent. Only the Old Spanish liturgy kept this principle of the choice of verse from the same source as the responsory itself.

3. When two, three, or even four responsories are taken from the same psalm, the incipit of this psalm is cited only in one verse; the others take another passage from the psalm.

4. When a psalm is divided into two or even three parts by a *diapsalma*, the psalm verse immediately following the *diapsalma* is considered a possible incipit for a responsory (for example, *Venite filii* [Ps 33:12]) or for a verse.

Cassiodorus, a contemporary of Saint Benedict, adopted the solution of a pause after the *diapsalma* for his monastery of Vivarium in Calabria: "Nos divisiones congrue faciemus ubicumque in psalmis diapsalma potuerit inveniri" (We must conveniently make a pause wherever we find a diapsalma in the psalms).[31]

---

30. *De ecclesiasticis officiis* 1.7, ed. Christopher Lawson, CCSL 113 (Turnhout: Brepols, 1989), 7–8. The two texts of this work and the parallel citations of Isidore's *Etymologiae* 6.19.7–8, were cited in the eighth-century *Liber glossarum*. See Huglo, "Recherche sur la psalmodie," 362.

31. *Expositio psalmorum, In psalmis praefatio* 11 (PL 70:17B; Adriaen, CCSL 97–98, 14–15); Cassiodorus, *Explanation of the Psalms*, trans. Patrick Gerard Walsh, Ancient Christian Writers 51–53 (New York: Newman Press, 1990).

The last rule and the solution of Cassiodorus help us to understand the terms used by Hilary of Poitiers (d. ca. 367) in his *Tractatus in Psalmos*: "The *diapsalma* inserted into several psalms is destined to indicate the beginning of a change of person or of meaning, thanks to a change of the musical mode; if a *diapsalma* appears somewhere, one must understand that one must change to another mode of the theory of music" after the pause, as was mentioned by Cassiodorus. From this text we can interpret what Hilary of Poitiers meant by the terms *ars musica* and *modus (modulus) musicus*.[32] A declaration of this kind by an author who had spent five years in the East, and who consequently knew the rules of Eastern antiphonal psalmody following the modes κατὰ τὸν τῶν ἀντιφώνων τρόπον,[33] must be seriously considered.

THE STRUCTURE OF AMBROSIAN PSALMODY

The Ambrosian psalmody was originally responsorial psalmody, whose tenor was on the same degree as the final of the *responsorium*. In the diatonic vocal scale, the choice of the final and of the psalmodic tenor could be any one of the four scale degrees of the tetrachord of the finals: D E F G. For example, in the antiphon *Cor meum* (see ex. 6.2), the tenor is established on the same degree as the final, that is, on the pitch a, but one could just as well have notated the chant a fourth lower, with a final on E, in this case, a vestige of responsorial psalmody.

Table 6.5 presents the structure of the later Ambrosian antiphonal psalmody, established according to the synthesis of the *Cantus psalmorum* made by Dom Suñol in the *Liber vesperalis ecclesiae Mediolanensis* on the basis of examples of psalmody found in the oldest Ambrosian antiphoners. Suñol's first observation concerns the ambitus of the melodies that span the tetrachord of the finals, D E F G, but sometimes spill over into the higher tetrachord, a b c d.

---

32. "Diapsalma uero, quod interiectum plurimis psalmis est, cognoscendum est, demutationem aut personae aut sensus sub conuersione modi musici inchoari: ut, sicubi diapsalma intercesserit, aut aliquid aliud dici, aut etiam ab altero dici, aut in altero artis musicae modulo cantari intellegendum sit." *S. Hilarii episcopi Pictaviensis: Tractatus super psalmos*, ed. Anton Zingerle, CSEL 22 (Vienna: G. Freytag, 1891), 18 (*Instructio psalmorum* 23).

33. See note 22 above. One can observe here that the Greek text that was translated in the fifth or sixth century into the Latin "antiphones" is in fact a *troparion*, followed by the sign of its mode: Ἦχ or πλ. See Egon Wellesz, *A History of Byzantine Music and Hymnography*, 2nd ed. (Oxford: Clarendon Press, 1961), 171.

Table 6.5. The Structure of the Ambrosian Psalmody

	Intonation	Tenor	Number of termination formulas	Possible degrees for the final note of the termination formula	Related Gregorian Tone
1st series of ps. for antiphons with final D	F G a C (D)E G C D F C D E	a G F E	14 14 14 _4_ 46	a G F D G F E D G F E D C E D C	I II
2nd series of ps. for antiphons with final E	G a c G a ♮ E G a E F G C D F C D E	c ♮ a G F E	3 4 14 16 8 _6_ 51	a a G E a G F E D G F E D C E D C E D C	III IV
3rd series of ps. for antiphons with final F	F a c ♮ F G a F G C D F	c a G F	12 3 11 _1_ 27	d c ♮ a G G F G F E D C D	V VI
4th series of ps. for antiphons with final G	G ♮ d G a c G a ♮ G a	d c ♮ a	16 10 3 _5_ 34	d c ♮ G c ♮ a G ♮ G ♮ a G F	VII VIII
		Overall Total:	158		

Adapted from Michel Huglo, "Recherches sur la psalmodie alternée à deux choeurs," *Revue bénédictine* 116, no. 2 (2006): 361.

For the antiphons on the finals D and E, the intonation of the psalm tone passes by the subtonic; for the antiphons with F and G as finals, the intonation leaves the final of the antiphons directly, except in one antiphon among the chants with their final on F.

The dominant of the psalmody, or the psalmodic tenor, is most often a third or a fourth above the final, but sometimes a fifth: one finds, in the last column of table 6.5, a rather vague connection between the psalm tones of Ambrosian chant and the eight tones of Gregorian plainchant: the concordance is approximate, because the Gregorian psalm tones include an embellished medial cadence and also offer a variety of closing formulas of a greater ambitus than those of the Ambrosian chant.

The flexibility of the Ambrosian psalm system allowed it to be adapted to the antiphons of a much larger ambitus that were added in later times, which sometimes cannot fully inscribe themselves into the rigid structures of the oktoechos. Thus the recitation of the psalm can be established on one of the seven tenors extending from E to d. In general, the tenor is chosen according to the highest note of the antiphon: since the ambitus of the antiphons of the Psalter is often reduced to a third or a fourth, one only rarely finds a fifth between the final and the tenor, an essential condition for the authentic tones of the oktoechos.

At the medial cadence of the verse in Ambrosian psalmody, as in Old Spanish psalmody, the choir makes a short pause. This solution avoids the imposition of a higher note as embellishment, which might not be part of the antiphon melody itself.

Often, the final psalm differentia is reduced to a drop of one degree at the last syllable of the verse, thus psalmody is reduced to its simplest expression, since the medial cadence of the verse is a short pause, without a melodic flex. According to Augustine, in the church of Alexandria Bishop Athanasius (d. 373) "caused the reader of the psalm to sound it forth with so little warbling of the voice, as that it was nearer to speaking than to singing."[34]

Some antiphons of the Milanese *Psalterium per hebdomadas*[35] have a pentatonic structure (C [D] F G a), as in other Mediterranean repertories: for example, *Timentes autem, Exsurgam diluculo, In te speravi*. In this case, the psalmodic tenor is established on the same degree as the highest pitch of the antiphon.

In several antiphons, the pentatonic structure is regularized at the end, by the cadences F–E–D or c–h–a, as, for example, in the antiphons *Mitte verbum tuum, Mitte manum tuam, Stellae et lumen, Quam admirabile, Ab insurgentibus*, and others. Another cadential formula (C–E–D) exists for the same reason, in *Sagittas parvulorum, Ipse tamquam sponsus*, and others.

Finally, in the case of an intonation beginning on a high pitch and descending to the final, as, for example, in the antiphons *Vovete et reddite, Non vos derelinquam*, and *Psallite Deo nostro*, the differentia of the psalmody is reversed (c–c–c–c–cd).

In fact, the antiphonal psalmody of the Ambrosian *Psalterium per hebdomadas* can be inscribed within the two disjunct tetrachords D E F G / a h c d, which form the basis of the later scales of Eastern and Western chant: the ratio of the intervals was calculated by Porphyry (d. 305 in Rome) in his commentary on the *Timaios* of Plato (ex. 6.3).[36]

---

34. "Tam modico flexu vocis faciebat sonare lectorem psalmi, ut pronuntianti vicinior esset quam canenti." Augustine, *Confessiones* 10.33, ed. William Watts, Loeb Classical Library 27 (Cambridge, Mass.: Harvard University Press, 1996), 166–167.

35. The cited antiphons are taken from the diplomatic edition by Terence Bailey and Paul Merkley, *The Melodic Tradition of the Ambrosian Office Antiphons*, Musicological Studies 50/2 (Ottawa: Institute of Medieval Music, 1990), *Antiphonae in psalmos proprios*.

36. Porphyry's commentary on the *Timaios* of Plato is lost, but it was reconstructed after the explicit citations of Macrobius, in his "Commentaries on the Dream of Scipio" (ca. 420/430 CE),

EXAMPLE 6.3

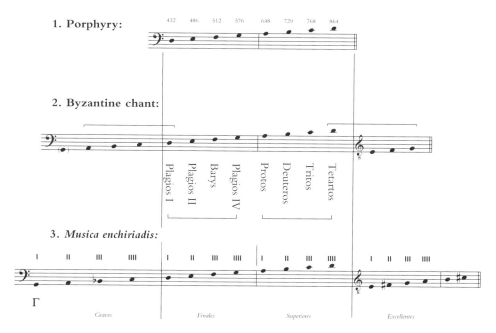

1. Sodano, ed., *Porphyrii in Platonis Timaeum* (see note 36).

2. Byzantine chant: Jørgen Raasted, *Intonation Formulas and Modal Signatures in Byzantine Musical Manuscripts*, Monumenta Musicae Byzantinae, Subsidia 7 (Copenhagen: Munksgaard, 1966) 199; Oliver Strunk, "The Tonal System of Byzantine Chant," *The Musical Quarterly* 28 (1942): 199.

3. *Musica enchiriadis*: Hans Schmid, ed. *Musica et Scolica enchiriadis*, 6 (Munich: C. H. Beck, 1981); Nancy Phillips, "'Musica' *and* 'Scolica enchiriadis': *The Literary, Theoretical, and Musical Sources*" (PhD diss., New York University, 1984), 163–200.

The difference between the old responsorial psalmody and the new antiphonal psalmody results from these observations: now the antiphon is no longer a brief refrain leading to a psalm tenor on the same pitch as its final, but it has become an extended composition with three, four, or more phrases, requiring a melody rising to a higher reciting tone, which, in turn, determines the choice of a tenor that is higher, but which still concords with the final.

---

by Angelo Raffaele Sodano, *Porphyrii in Platonis Timaeum Commentariorum fragmenta* (Naples, Instituto della Stampa, 1964). The diagrams have come down to us from the brief treatise on music interpolated into the Visigothic manuscripts of the *Etymologiae* or *Origines* of Isidore of Seville. On this treatise, see Michel Huglo, "The *Musica Isidori* Tradition in Iberian Peninsula," *Hispania vetus: Musical-Liturgical Manuscripts; From Visigothic Origins to the Franco-Roman Transition (9–12 Centuries)*, ed. Susana Zapke (Madrid: BBVA Fundación, 2008), 61–92.

The scale of the responsorial psalmody is limited to two tetrachords, whereas the scale of either the simple or the ornate antiphonal psalmody—the latter that of the nocturnal responsories, graduals and *psalmelli*—can, following the situation, be extended to a higher pitch or a lower pitch, provided it does not surpass the interval of a twelfth.

During the passage of responsorial psalmody to antiphonal psalmody, the melody of the *responsorium* remained unchanged, but the pitch of the recitation of the psalmody was chosen with respect to the melodic constitution of the antiphon, which developed around the final, either moved higher or lower. Thus the scale of the chant was extended by the simple reproduction of the original two tetrachords at the lower or upper fifth.[37]

Eventually, the sources of the Ambrosian texts ranged from all of the books of the Bible to free compositions that were sometimes borrowed from the old Gallican liturgy[38] or translated from Greek. As was the case with the hymnary, the repertoire of chants became progressively larger without the suppression of previous acquisitions. Nevertheless, in the chant for the mass borrowed from the Gallican or Roman repertories,[39] the melodies were modified in the style proper to Ambrosian chant, notably by the imposition of the Ambrosian intonation and cadence in place of the "foreign" formulas.[40]

Indeed, Milan never accepted the psalm tones with two different reciting tones (e.g., the *tonus peregrinus*) or the ornamented psalm tones coming from Gaul for the Benedictus and the Magnificat: on Christmas Day in Milan, the Magnificat antiphon *Beata es que credidisti* is still sung to a pentatonic melody (ex. 6.4).

EXAMPLE 6.4

Be – a – ta es quae cre – di – di – sti. E u o u a e.

---

37. *Musica enchiriadis*, cap. IV; *Quare unum solum tetrachordum sub finalibus sit et duo supra* (Schmid, ed., *Musica et scolica enchiriadis*, 8); Why only one tetrachord is under the finals and two are above (Raymond Erickson, trans., *Musica enchiriadis and Scolica enchiriadis* [New Haven: Yale, 1995], 4).

38. For example, the antiphon *Venite populi*, preserved in a palimpsest of the eighth century. See Huglo et al., *Fonti e paleografia*, 6, nos. 2 and 124, and Terence Bailey, ed., *The Transitoria of the Ambrosian Mass Edited from Three Sources*, Collected Works 21 (Ottawa: Institute of Mediaeval Music, 2002), 98–99.

39. Compare Dom Jean Claire, "Vecchio Milanese," *Studi gregoriani* 21 (2005): 7–145.

40. Huglo et al., *Fonti e paleografia*, 130–132.

I wish to thank Dom Jean Mallet (Solesmes) for providing information about the Ambrosian Psalter and biblical canticles; Joseph Dyer for his comments on this text; Barbara Haggh, for translating and editing this article; Evan MacCarthy, for collating the information presented in table 6.3 with the contents of the Ambrosian antiphoners in the Houghton Library; Thomas Lin, for creating the musical examples; and Matthew Mugmon, for creating table 6.5 from my typescript.

Appendix A

DESCRIPTION OF THE OLDEST AMBROSIAN PSALTERS

Munich, Bayerische Staatsbibliothek, Clm 343. Psalter and Hymnary of the Ambrosian liturgy.

236 ff., parchment, 295 × 174 mm <150 × 90 mm>, 20 lines per page. Binding of leather without decoration. Caroline minuscule by one hand of the third quarter of the ninth century; written in Milan. Corrections of the twelfth century (Bernhard Bischoff, *Katalog der festländischen Handschriften des neunten Jahrhunderts*, Teil 2, *Laon-Paderborn* (Wiesbaden: Harrassowitz, 2004), 221, n° 2925. Provenance: Augsburg (fol. 1r).

CONTENTS

1. Prologues and paintings

fol. 1v   Prologus Psalmorum: *Vt reprobare superflua et inserere congrua . . .*

fol. 3r   De vitiis: *Quattuor namque modis in Scripturis vitia . . .*

fol. 6r   De notis: *Quinque sunt notae quas in hoc psalterio depinximus . . .*

fol. 9v   Incipit dicta sancti Augustini episcopi: *Quid sint psalmorum virtutes . . .*

fol. 10v   Incipit expositio psalmorum vel litterarum quae diversorum capita cognoscitur haec prefatio . . .

fol. 11r   *Psalterium dicitur a psallentium multorum modulatione voce. Quia et ipse David tenens psalterium in manibus . . .* (Explicit) *. . . qui finem ita habent et ita munies in fine libri fiat, fiat.*

fol. 12v   Painting in frame with crisscross: David, under arch, playing crwth with his musicians Asaph, Aeman, Aethan and Idithun. See Dom Paul Blanchon-Lasserve, *Écriture et enluminure des manuscrits du IXe au XIIe siècles* (Sablé-sur-Sarthe: Abbaye St.-Pierre de Solesmes, 1927; Lophem-lez-Bruges: Abbaye de St.-André, 1931), pl. VI; and Pietro Toesca, *La pittura e la miniatura nella Lombardia dai piu antichi monumenti alla meta del Quattrocento* (Milan: Einaudi, 1966), Tav. 46.

fol. 13r   *David filius Hiesse cum esset in regno suo, quattuor elegit qui psalmos facerent, id est Asaph, Aeman, Aethan and Idithun . . .* (short commentary on the painting).

fol. 14v   [Explicit] . . . *Diapsalma est «semper,»* quod est fiat, fiat, quod est requies, quod
              est spiritus pausat, quod est spiritus pausatio, quod est fiat, fiat, hoc est Semper.

              [In the *Psalterium iuxta Haebreos,* the word *semper* is the translation for
              Diapsalma in the Greek Psalter of the Septuagint.]

fol. 15r   Versiculi Hieronimi presbyteri: *Psallere qui docuit dulci modulatione sanctis …*
              [sanctos, *edd.*]. Donatien de Bruyne, *Préfaces de la Bible latine* (Namur: A.
              Godenne, 1920), 66; Weakland, "The Office Antiphons," 76.

2. The Psalter

fol. 17v   On full page, inside of a rectangular frame, with interlacing: INCIPIT/
              LIBER/PSALMO/RUM (Toesca, *La pittura,* Tav. 47).

fol. 18r   On full page, inside of a rectangular frame, with interlacing: tall *B*, initial
              of Psalm 1: *Beatus vir qui non habiit in consilio impiorum.*

fol. 18v   Here and in all following psalms, the verses are written *per cola et commata*;
              the second part of the verse, after the mediant, is written under the
              first part at the end of the psalm: ORATIO, *Effice nos Domine tamquam
              fructuosissimum lignum* . . . This collect and the others written at the end
              of each psalm are edited in *The Psalter Collects,* with introduction, critical
              apparatus, and index by Dom Brou, from the papers of Dom André
              Wilmart (see note 2), p. 48. (This witness to the "Roman Series" is
              omitted by Brou and Wilmart, who cite only Vat. lat. 82 and 83).

              The short title of each psalm is written in red uncials; texts edited by
              Pierre Salmon, *Les* tituli psalmorum *des manucrits latins,* Études liturgiques
              3 (Paris: Cerf, 1959), 151–186. Series 6 follows MSS Vat. lat. 82 and lat. 83;
              the Munich manuscript was not considered here.

              The beginning of each *deguria,* i.e., Pss 11, 21, 31, etc., is indicated with
              one colored initial filling 4–5 lines; the first of each group of fifty
              psalms, i.e., Ps 51 (fol. 79r) and Ps 101 (fol. 137v) did not receive special
              decoration: see Toesca, *La pittura,* Tav. 48 [Ps.131], and Rainer Kashnitz,
              "Frühe Initial Psalter," in F. O. Büttner, ed. *The Illuminated Psalter,* 151–
              152, and ills. 115 [Ps 31], 116 [Ps 61], 117 [Ps 71], 118 [Ps 131].

              The *diapsalma* inside seventy psalms (see above, p. 113-114) is indicated in
              small capitals.

fol. 198r   In the margin of Pss 148 and 149, the letters AL(leluia) are probably a
              witness to the *alleluiaticum* used in Gaul at the end of lauds (see Aurelian
              of Réôme, *Musica disciplina,* cap. XX, ed. Lawrence Gushee, Corpus

scriptorum de musica 21 [Rome: American Institute of Musicology, 1975], 133).

fol. 200v Ps 151, *extra numerum, Pusillus eram inter fratres meos*, is entitled: *Admonetur civitas Dei ut de mundi ambitu congregata Domino, laudes et ore cantet et anima* . . .

3. The Biblical Canticles

fol. 201r Canticum Esaiae Prophetae: *De nocte vigilat* (Is 26:9–20).

Oratio Annae pro Samuhel propheta: *Confirmatum est cor meum* (1 Sm 2:1–10)

Canticum Abbachuch prophetae: *Domine audivi auditum tuum* (Hb 3:2–14), with *diapsalma* after the v/3, 9 et 13, translated here by *semper* (see fol. 14r).

Canticum Jonae prophetae: *Clamavi ad Dominum* (Jon 2:3–9).

Canticum Deuteronomi: *Attende caelum et loquar* (Dt 32:1–43).

Canticum Moysi prophetae: *Cantemus Domino, gloriose enim* (Ex 15:1–19).

Canticum Zachariae prophetae: *Benedictus Dominus Deus Israel* (Lk 1:68–79)

Oratio sanctae Mariae: *Magnificat* (Lc 1, 46–54).

Hymnum trium puerorum: *Benedictus es Domine* (Dn 3:52–56).

Item alium himnum trium puerorum: *Benedicite omnia opera Domini Domino* (Dn 3:57–88).

See Heinrich Schneider, *Die altlateinische biblischen Cantica*, Texte und Arbeiten 29–30 (Beuron: Erzabtei, 1938), 99–126; Philippe Bernard, "Le Cantique des trois enfants (Dan. 3, 52-90): Les répertoires occidentaux dans l'Antiquité tardive et le Haut Moyen-Age," *Musica e Storia* 1 (1993): 231–272; Ruth Steiner, "The Canticle of the Three Children as a Chant of the Roman Mass," *Schweizer Jahrbuch für Musikwissenschaft*, n.F., 2 (1982): 81–90, reprinted in Ruth Steiner, *Studies in Gregorian Chant* (Aldershot: Ashgate, 1999), article 17.

4. The Hymnal

fol. 211v–212v Ymnum sanctae Trinitatis *Te Deum laudamus* (critical edition by Frost, "*Te Deum laudamus*: The Milan Text," 192–194, and idem, "Notes on the *Te Deum*: the Final Verses," 250–256: the last verse of the Milanese

> *Te Deum* (even in the antiphonaries) is taken from the Canticle of Daniel,
> 3:52: *Benedictus es Domine Deus patrum nostrorum . . . Amen.*

fol. 213r–231v   Hymnal (42 hymns). See Marie Hélène Jullien, "Les sources de
la tradition ancienne des hymnes attribuées à saint Ambroise," *Revue
d'histoire des textes* 19 (1989): 74 (siglum *Ma*), and Giacomo Baroffio, "La
tradizione musicale degli Inni di sant'Ambrogio," in *Studia Ambrosiana:
Ricerche e studi su Ambrogio e la sua epoca* 2 (2008): 251–261.

fol. 232r   Incipit Expositio catholicae fidei Athanasii: *Quicumque vult salvus esse . . .*
Henricus Denzinger; *Enchiridion symbolorum*, 34th ed. (Barcelona: Herder,
1967), 40–42.

fol. 234r   Incipit exorcismus sancti Ambrosii episcopi: *Omnipotens Domine Verbum
Dei Patris, Christe Jesus . . .*

Vatican City, Biblioteca Apostolica Vaticana, MS Vat. lat. 82.

258 ff., parchment, 216 × 156 mm. Caroline minuscule (last third of the ninth
century, according to Bernhard Bischoff). Notation with points and accents on
the psalter antiphons added in the fourteenth century (Henry Marriott Bannister,
Monumenti Vaticani di paleografia musicale latina [Leipzig: Harrassowitz, 1913], no. 287).
Provenance: Pontida (since the fourteenth century).

Same content as Clm 343, but 48 hymns (fols. 217v–242v), instead of 42 as in Clm
343 (Jullien, "Les sources," 75). There follows the *Quicumque vult* (Athanasian Creed)
and the *Exorcismus: Consideratio psalmorum in diversis causis* and *Confessio peccatorum.*

Description: Marco Vattasso and P. Franchi De' Cavalieri, *Bibliothecae Apostolicae
Vaticanae Codices Vaticani latini*, vol. 1 (Rome: Typis Polyglottis Vaticanis, 1902), 76–78;
Monumenta Germaniae Historica, Epistolae, VI, 201 (MS V_1); Brou, *Psalter Collects*, 48
(M1); Frost, *"Te Deum,"* 192; Klaus Gamber, *Codices liturgici latini antiquiores*, vol. 1
(Fribourg: Universitätsverlag, 1968), no. 591; Huglo et al., *Fonti e paleografia*, 7, no.
4; Salmon, *Tituli psalmorum*, series 6, MS X; Salmon, *Les manuscrits liturgiques latins
de la Bibliothèque Vaticane,* vol. 1: *Psautiers, Hymnaires*, Studi e testi 251 (Vatican City:
Biblioteca Apostolica Vaticano, 1968), 30, no. 56; Schneider, *Altlateinische Cantica*, 99.

Vatican City, Biblioteca Apostolica Vaticana, MS Vat. lat. 83.

VI + 232 ff., parchment, 250 × 177 mm. Caroline minuscule (last third of the ninth century, according to Bernhard Bischoff). Provenance: *In sancto Victore ad ulmum* (f. VIr).

Painting, Franco-Saxon decoration, interlacing and beaks of ducks; David, under Roman vault, playing harp, with four musicians (Toesca, *La pittura*, tav. 45).

Same content as Clm 343, but with additional *Ordo officii ferialis ambrosianus* (fols. 231v, fifteenth century): cf. Huglo et al., *Fonti e paleografia*, 7, no. 5.

Description: Vattasso and De' Cavalieri, *Bibliothecae Apostolicae Vaticanae Codices Vaticani latini*, vol. 1 (1902), 78–79; *Monumenta Germaniae Historica, Epistolae*, VI, 201 (MS V$_2$); Brou, *Psalter Collects*, 48 (M³); Frost, "*Te Deum*," 192; Gamber, *CLLA*, I, 1, n° 592; Jullien, "Les sources," 75; Salmon, *Tituli psalmorum*, series 6, MS Y; Salmon, *Les manuscrits liturgiques latins de la Bibliothèque Vaticane*, series 6, MS Y; Schneider, *Altlateinische Cantica*, 99.

Christmas Masses in the
Ambrosian Liturgy

Terence Bailey

CHRISTMAS WAS NOT AMONG THE EARLIEST OF THE CHRISTIAN FESTIVALS. It is known to have been celebrated in Rome—no doubt from the beginning with a special mass—before 354, for it is documented locally[1] in that year, during the pontificate of Liberius I, who held office from 352 until 366. It was probably only shortly afterward[2] that Ambrose's older sister Marcellina became a nun in Rome, on which occasion (the day was "natalis Christi," as it happens, but whether this was December 25 or January 6 is uncertain) the pope delivered the sermon reported by Ambrose.[3] He and Marcellina were born Christian into a well-connected Roman family that was obviously closely associated with the highest Roman clergy, and we can be sure that Ambrose was kept aware of liturgical developments in the city where he lived from about 354 to 370, even after he moved north to become governor of the province of Emilia and Liguria. And since he later gave assurances that in liturgical matters he "followed in all things the form and fashion of Rome,"[4] it seems safe to assume that a Christmas mass was instituted in Milan soon after Ambrose became bishop in 374.[5] Since his predecessor was an Arian it seems unlikely that the festival on December 25 was introduced there in the twenty years prior to Ambrose's ordination.

While any number of masses may be said on a single occasion in a single church by different priests, there are few exceptions to the ancient and understandable limitation that the same officiant may say mass only once a day. Christmas was such a special case. The Gelasian Sacramentary (which may record

---

1. In the Calendar of Philocalus (*Patrologia Latina*, vol. 13, col. 675; Josef Strzygowski, *Die Kalenderbilder des Chronographen von Jahre 354* [Berlin, 1888]).

2. Assuming Marcellina was born about 330.

3. *De virginibus* 3.1, in *Patrologia Latina*, vol. 16, col. 219. Joseph Dyer has kindly mentioned Hans Förster's critical assessment of this sermon, *Die Feier der Geburt Christi in der alten Kirche* (Tübingen: Mohr Siebeck, 2000), 174.

4. "Ecclesia romana . . . cuius typum in omnibus sequimur et formam." *De sacramentis* 3.1.5, ed. Johannes Quasten, *Monumenta eucharistica et liturgica vetustissima*, Florilegium Patristicum 7 (Bonn: Peter Hanstein, 1936), 152. Ambrose's authorship of the treatise is widely accepted.

5. The date is sometimes given as 373.

practices as old as the sixth century) includes three masses for December 25. Two of these might be explained by the practices of Jerusalem, where in 385 the pilgrim usually known as Egeria mentioned a double, episcopal, celebration of the birth of Jesus—at night in Bethlehem (tradition has it that Jesus was born at night) and during the day in Jerusalem. The second of the three masses in Rome can be explained by local circumstances: it began as a diplomatic courtesy, celebrated, presumably by the pope, for the resident emissaries of the Byzantine government in their official chapel on the Palatine, the Church of Saint Anastasia, whose feast day was December 25. This mass was instituted, obviously, only after the reconquest of the city in 552 by Narses.

While three Christmas masses—traditionally in the night, at dawn, and during the day—are found circa 800 in the earliest Gregorian books, for example, in all those of Hesbert's *Sextuplex* edition,[6] there is no trace of extra masses in the oldest Ambrosian books.[7] This is somewhat surprising, considering the many Gregorian reforms accepted in Milan after Charlemagne's conquest of the city in 774 and in light of the obvious predilection of the Milanese for Christmas—a festival whose liturgy was elaborated in other ways to a quite extraordinary degree. Extra Ambrosian masses were eventually added, at first only one, which allows for speculation that the prompting might have been the customs of Bethlehem and Jerusalem, and then two, more obviously explained as owing to Roman influence. In the end, four Christmas masses were sung, and as many as six sets of mass items can be documented.

The mass of Christmas Eve, first detailed in the *Manuale Ambrosianum*[8] in the early eleventh century but certainly very much older, was celebrated *during* vespers[9] on the twenty-fourth of December (a similar vigils mass is entered for Epiphany).[10]

6. René-Jean Hesbert, *Antiphonale missarum sextuplex* (1935; repr., Rome: Herder, 1985).

7. According to Antonio Ceriani, a scholar whose knowledge went beyond liturgical books (until his death in 1907 he was prefect of the Biblioteca Ambrosiana) nothing from the ninth century attests to extra masses on December 25; in the tenth century there is evidence only for that of Saint Anastasia—not, of course, a mass "of the Lord." Magistretti (who cites Ceriani) notes that the Mass of Saint Anastasia was omitted from the Ambrosian missal only in 1499 (*Beroldus sive ecclesiae ambrosianae Mediolanensis kalendarium et ordines*, ed. Marco Magistretti [Milan, 1894], 195 n. 138).

8. The *Manuale*, which contains the complete texts and some rubrics for both mass and office, was edited by Marco Magistretti, *Manuale Ambrosianum*, part 1, *Psalterium et Kalendarium* (Milan, 1905); part 2, *Manuale Ambrosianum ex codice saec. xi olim in usum canonicae Vallis Travaliae* (1904; repr., Nendeln, Liechtenstein: Kraus Reprint, 1971).

9. Vespers began with the usual items (the lucernarium, hymn, *responsorium post hymnum*, etc.) and concluded in the usual way with the *Magnificat* and final observances in both baptisteries.

10. See the provisions for the vigil of Pentecost (*Manuale*, 271), where the chant between the readings was an alleluia and where additional mass items are entered. Vigils masses without these extra items were a feature of all saints' feasts celebrated at stations away from the cathedral. Other "evening" (actually afternoon) masses, *following* stational vespers, are also to be found. I

Festivals of the saints or "of the Lord" began in the evening (notionally sundown) the day before their assigned calendar date. This, of course, is in keeping with the practice of the Jews, who similarly observe the Sabbath from Friday evening.[11]

Vigils were occasions of penance in preparation for the celebration that followed, and the mass was simple, indeed, greatly abbreviated: the only items specified on Christmas Eve (and at first vespers of Epiphany) are a reading from the Epistles, a reading from the Gospels, and, between them, a cantus—the counterpart of the Roman tract (on penitential occasions the alleluia that is usual before a Gospel reading would not be appropriate). Since for such observances the word *missa* was used,[12] we must conclude that the Eucharist was distributed, although this was perhaps consecrated earlier,[13] as in the Roman Mass of the Presanctified. (I should make the general observation here that the directions in the later Ambrosian service books are not to be trusted as indications of earlier usage: so much changed, especially after the reforms of the sixteenth century.)

Penitential masses on the eve of great feasts belong certainly to the oldest stratum of the Ambrosian liturgy, but the festive mood of what is popularly the most joyous of feasts came later to color even its vigils. There was at least one attempt to elaborate the vespers mass of Christmas Eve, to change its character by increasing the solemnity of the occasion. In what is probably the oldest Ambrosian antiphoner,[14] British Library Add. MS 34209, dated uncertainly to the first part of the twelfth century, text cues for an offerenda, a confractorium, and a transitorium were entered[15] in addition to the usual cantus (*Qui regis Israel intende*), although no ingressa[16] and no *antiphona post evangelium* are indicated. I say *were* entered because these additions were subsequently erased. It would seem that a local elaboration entirely typical of the development of the Ambrosian liturgy was overruled by a later, more conservative, authority.

hope soon to finish a paper on the Ambrosian masses *ante*, *in*, and *post vesperis*.

11. Although Christians normally began the celebration of saints' festivals the evening before the festival date, ordinary Sundays or weekdays were seen to begin with the night office, some time after midnight, and to end with compline.

12. The learned editor of the *Manuale* has added the words "ad missam" and "post missam" in the case of Christmas and Epiphany, but see *Manuale*, 253, 260, 268. Ambrose uses the word *missa* in a letter to Marcellina (Letter 20, 4–5; *Epistula*, ed. Otto Faller and Michaela Zelzer, Corpus Scriptorum Ecclesiasticorum Latinorum 82/1–3 [Vienna, 1968–90]), where there is no doubt that it meant the Eucharistic service.

13. The vespers mass included none of the chants (*antiphona post evangelium*, offerenda, confractorium) usually associated with the preparation of the Eucharist.

14. At least one fragment is older: Vatican City, Biblioteca Apostolica Vaticana, Ottob. lat. 3. See below, note 24.

15. Between the first and second staves on p. 50. The chant incipits are not legible. As far as I know, such cues are found in no other source.

16. As the celebrant would already be in the choir for vespers, an ingressa was not necessary.

There is general agreement in all Ambrosian service books about the items for the main mass sung on Christmas morning (*mane ad missam*) in the principal (winter) cathedral: the ingressa, psalmellus and verse, the alleluia and verse (sung with extra, very lengthy *melodiae*, including the *francigena* melisma, about which much has been written), an *antiphona ante evangelium*, *antiphona post evangelium*, offerenda and verse, confractorium, and transitorium. All these chants are proper to the occasion, and two of them (the *antiphona ante evangelium* and the extra *melodiae*) are unusual items, sung only on the greatest of feasts.

The *Manuale* is the earliest of the service books to detail the Ambrosian liturgy. In all but one of the copies edited by Magistretti, the main mass is the only one mentioned. However, in what is probably the oldest of all,[17] dated (uncertainly) about 1000, cues are entered for the items of one additional mass *in nocte sancta*. These items are an ingressa, an Old Testament lesson, a psalmellus and verse, a reading from the Epistles, an alleluia verse (it goes without saying that the alleluia itself was also sung),[18] a Gospel reading, an offerenda, a confractorium, and a transitorium (but no *antiphona post evangelium*):

> *Hodie nobis caelorum rex* (ingressa)
> *Salvator noster descendit* V. *Regnum teneo [virginitatis]* (psalmellus)
> *Puer natus est* (*versus in alleluia*)
> *Hodierni diei [sollemnitas]* (offerenda)
> *Per viscera [misericordiae]* (confractorium)
> *Gaudeamus omnes [fideles]* (transitorium)

All of these chants are borrowed, and most are used transgressively (that is, without respect for their genre): the ingressa is properly an *antiphona in choro*; the psalmellus was sung earlier at vespers; the alleluia verse, in spite of its text ("A boy is born") and the offerenda (which is really an *antiphona ad crucem*) are from the feast of Saint Stephen; and the confractorium and transitorium are properly a processional antiphons (*psallendae*) sung on different occasions during Christmas Week. Such assignments demonstrate that the extra mass, *Hodie nobis* (henceforth I refer to mass complexes by their ingressa), obviously a late addition to the liturgy, was compiled when niceties were no longer observed.

An extra Christmas mass, *not* the one in the *Manuale*, is detailed in the Ambrosian ordinal, a work compiled shortly after the death of Archbishop Olrich in 1125[19] but certainly based on older documents:

---

17. Milan, Biblioteca Ambrosiana, MS Trotti 414 (Magistretti's MS S).

18. Which alleluia (there were only ten used in the Ambrosian liturgy) would have been known to the singers from the verse assigned. See Terence Bailey, *The Ambrosian Alleluias* (Engelfied Green, England: Plainsong and Mediaeval Music Society, 1983).

19. For the dating, see *Beroldus*, Magistretti's *Praefatio*, p. ix; cf. *Dictionnaire d'archéologie chrétienne et de liturgie* (ed. Fernand Cabrol, 1907–53), vol. 11/2, c. 1083.

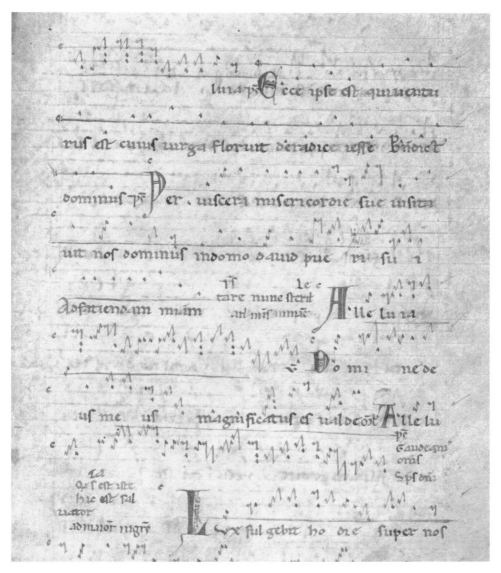

FIGURE 7.1   Cambridge, Mass., Harvard University, Houghton Library, MS Lat 388, fol. 54r, 20 × 16

> *Laetare nunc sterilis* (ingressa)
> *Domine Deus meus* (versus in alleluia)
> *Gaudeamus omnes [fideles]* (antiphona post evangelium)
> *Spiritus Domini super me* (offerenda)
> *Quis est iste qui venit* (confractorium)
> *Hic est salvator quem* (transitorium)

In this instance an *antiphona post evangelium* is included, but no Old Testament reading or concomitant psalmellus.

The extra mass found in the ordinal is similarly a late confection of borrowed pieces: *Laetare nunc* and *Spiritus Domini* are properly *antiphonae duplae*, sung earlier the same day at matins (it is not clear whether the second parts of these double-antiphons were sung at mass); *Domine Deus meus* is an alleluia verse from the *commune dominicarum*; *Quis est iste* is the *antiphona in choro* of the third Sunday of Advent; *Gaudeamus omnes*, as mentioned, is properly a psallenda.

The mass *Laetare nunc* was later to become standard. The earliest antiphoner known to include it is Houghton Library MS Lat 388,[20] one of the manuscripts recently purchased by Harvard University (fig. 7.1). On folio 54r, in the main hand, immediately following the *psallendae de baptisterio in aliud [baptisterium]*, which is the usual final entry for matins, is the rubric "ps" (psallenda), as though another processional antiphon were expected—the first indication that the copyist had encountered something unfamiliar—then a cue to *Laetare nunc sterilis*, a rubric, "ad missam in mane" (as though the main mass of Christmas morning were to follow), and only then the rest of the chants that with *Laetare nunc* make up the mass later called "missa in prima noctis," or simply "missa prima." For the alleluia, its verse, and the second alleluia with *melodiae*, the melodies are written out; all the other items are given as text cues (presumably, the alleluia is only written out for the sake of convenience: all the other chants needed for the mass are contained in the *pars hiemalis*, the current volume of the antiphoner; the *commune*, with the alleluia melismas,[21] would have been included in its companion volume, which is not known to have survived).

The mass *Laetare nunc*, with the designation "ad primam missam noctis natalis domini" has been added in the lower margin of two thirteenth-century antiphoners, MSS A and B, of the parish church (*chiesa plebana*) of Santo Stefano in Vimercate (a suburb of Milan).[22] But further cues for a second mass ("ad secundam

---

20. It is not found in Add. 34209, also of the twelfth century, nor in the other *pars hiemalis*, Milan, Biblioteca Capitolare, II.F.2.2, sometimes attributed to the thirteenth century, but more likely from the twelfth.

21. The *melodiae* vary substantially from one antiphoner to another; it is not possible to say, therefore, whether the melisma included in MS Lat 388 was in any way special to the occasion.

22. On folio 61v in both cases and in the same hand. Vimercate A and Vimercate B are obviously

missam") are also added (in the following list I have expanded the abbreviations without comment):

> *Dum medium silentium* (ingressa)
>
> *Venite [exsultemus Domino]* (versus in alleluia)
>
> *Gaudeamus omnes* (post evangelium)
>
> *O admirabile commercium* (offertorium)
>
> *Virgo hodie fidelis* (confractorium)
>
> *Magnificamus te Dei genetrix [. . . sancta][23]* (transitorium)

No psalmellus is cued; it seems there was no reading from the Old Testament.

As in the case of the masses *Hodie nobis* and *Laetare nunc*, the "missa secunda" has been cobbled together from borrowed chants. *Dum medium* is properly the ingressa for the Sunday following Epiphany. *Venite exsultemus* is an alleluia verse from the *commune dominicarum*. *Gaudeamus omnes* (which appears yet again) is a psallenda. *O admirabile commercium* and *Virgo hodie fidelis* are chants clearly imported from outside the Ambrosian orbit: they are widely disseminated in Gregorian books as antiphons for the Christmas season and for feasts of the Blessed Virgin. Before their co-option into the *missa secunda* of Christmas these two chants were used only peripherally in the Ambrosian liturgy, most prominently on the feast of the Annunciation as the twenty-seventh and twenty-ninth of the chants sung in the morning procession to the stational church, Santa Maria ad Circulum. Finally, *Magnificamus te dei* is the transitorium for Epiphany.

Let us reconsider the dates pertaining to the introduction and acceptance of the extra Christmas masses. The set of chants in the mass *Hodie nobis*—apparently a local compilation since it is not found in any later sources—was included in a copy of the *Manuale* dated to the end of the tenth or beginning of the eleventh century. As for the mass *Laetare nunc* in the ordinal, although Beroldus compiled his edition in the early twelfth century, we must assume from internal evidence (contradictions, inconsistencies) that a good deal of this book—probably most of it—is much older. Certain of Beroldus's contributions are obvious (in one case even signed, by way of an acrostic), but the directions for the mass *Laetare nunc* are in a style and format indistinguishable from that used throughout the ordinal: there is no reason to think it is an innovation of the twelfth century.

There is good evidence that the Ambrosian antiphoner existed before the

---

based on the same exemplar (there is no reason to think they were copied locally), although the pagination is not always exactly the same. It can be shown that neither is the direct source of the other. It has been suggested (ingeniously) that they were meant to be used together, one on either side of the choir. Although they were perhaps used in that way at Santo Stefano, this cannot have been the original intention, since the contents are not entirely identical.

23.   That the long version of this chant was intended is made clear by page references given with the text cues, references that show where the chant was written out in the antiphoner.

middle of the eleventh century—*how much* before remains conjectural.[24] The manuscript tradition of the Ambrosian antiphoner is relatively simple, and there are clear indications that the format of the archetype continued to be copied for centuries—even after the destruction of the winter cathedral and its baptistry in the fourteenth century made many of its rubrics obsolete. This standard format was the basis of Vimercate A and Vimercate B (indeed, for all antiphoners up to the end of the manuscript tradition). It is certain that only the masses at vigils on December 24 and during the day on December 25 were included in the archetype, and thus even late manuscripts modeled on it, such as the Vimercate antiphoners, have no room for the two extra masses, even though one of these was officially recognized fully a century and a half earlier in the ordinal compiled for the cathedral by Beroldus. This will explain why the additions in the Vimercate manuscripts had to be made in the margins.

MS Lat 388, on paleographical grounds, seems pretty clearly to belong to the twelfth century, most likely the mid-twelfth, as is given in the Harvard University Library catalog (http://discovery.lib.harvard.edu/). By the time it was copied, one extra mass, *Laetare nunc,* had become acceptable enough to be entered by some brave copyist—albeit with evidence of uncertainty—in its proper place. If two masses had been current, it is reasonable to think the other would also have been entered.

The first known appearance of the second mass, *Dum silentium,* is in the Vimercate antiphoners. Vimercate A and B and their companion volumes for the summer period (C and D) appear to have been written about the same time—from the style of their script and the few decorations of initial letters, in the thirteenth century. Evidence in one of the four may provide a more accurate date. On folio 226 of Vimercate D, after the last item of the antiphoner proper, a memorandum was added in a hand that seems contemporary with the event it recorded—a hand that is not unlike that of the added masses on folio 61v of the two winter antiphoners. The event noted in the memorandum is dated Thursday, September 6, 1272 ("anno domini MCCLXXII, die Jovis, sexto die Septembris"). If this is not a notice recopied into the book at a later date (which seems unlikely) we have a firm *terminus ante quem* for Vimercate D and an indication that the three Christmas masses that became the norm—they are found in later Ambrosian antiphoners,[25] from fourteenth century down to the edition of 1935—were not accepted everywhere before the third quarter of the thirteenth century.

---

24. Terence Bailey, "A Lost Ambrosian Antiphoner of Southern Italy," in *Plainsong and Medieval Music* 17 (2008): 1–22.

25. Angelo Rusconi, in table 4.2 of his contribution to this volume, lists some nonstandard assignments that he noted for the *missa in nocte* and the main mass *in die* in Mariano Comense (Como), MS A.

The Making and Breaking of Restrictive Chains:

A Closer Look at the Melodiae of Ambrosian Chant

Sasha Siem

Despite being indisputably the most eye-catching entries in Ambrosian manuscripts, very little research has been done, to my knowledge, on the so-called *melodiae*—lengthy melismas that span one or two folios though they set no more than two or three words. One of the more substantive references to the *melodiae* occurs in Terence Bailey's book on Ambrosian alleluias, in which he dedicates a section to the *melodiae* associated with alleluias.[1] Even a brief survey of Ambrosian manuscripts, however, reveals that *melodiae* do not only occur in association with alleluias but also with *responsoria cum infantibus*; unlike the former, most of which only state one *melodiae*, the latter always occur in pairs—*primae* and *secundae*.

The *melodiae* (as a genre in relation to the alleluias *and* within the body of Ambrosian chant as a whole) raise a plethora of unaddressed questions that beg discussion. Here I explore one in particular: in what way do the *melodiae primae* and *melodiae secundae* relate to each other?

I will consider the question with respect to a particular example, the *melodiae* at the end of the responsory *Vidi speciosam* and set to its final text, "Et lilia convalium." I chose this set of *melodiae primae* (M1) and *secundae* (M2) simply because it occurs in more than one manuscript available to me at the time of research, including one of the manuscripts under discussion at this conference—the comparison of multiple versions being a crucial means of assessing the specificity of my analytical observations—and because those observations are typical of all analyses of *melodiae* existing in multiple manuscripts that I have undertaken. "Et lilia" is used for feasts of the Blessed Virgin Mary and is found in Houghton Library MS Lat 389 for the feast of the Dedication, which is the source of all transcriptions in this article (see fig. 8.1). The following analysis focuses on two particular realizations of these *melodiae*, in MS Lat 389 and in the fourteenth-century manuscript Oxford, Bodleian Library, Lat. liturg. a 4.

---

1. Terence Bailey, *The Ambrosian Alleluias* (Englefield Green, Egham, Surrey: Plainsong & Medieval Music Society, 1983), 34. See also Roy Jesson's "Ambrosian Chant," in Willi Apel, *Gregorian Chant* (Bloomington: Indiana University Press, 1958), 465–483.

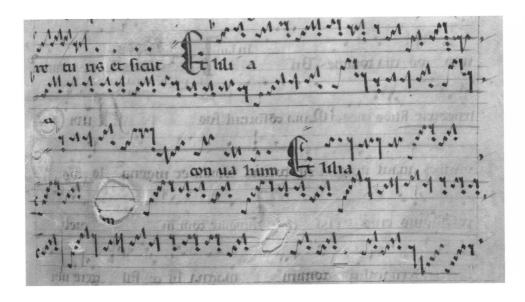

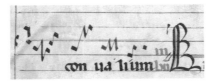

FIGURE 8.1   *Et lilia convalium*, Cambridge, Mass., Harvard University, Houghton Library, MS Lat 389, fols. 26r–26v, 10 × 17 / 2 × 4.5

Emancipation from Stepwise Motion

No comparison between parts of the *melodiae*—let alone between different versions—can be made before a close analysis of the first part. Perhaps the most noticeable feature of the *melodiae primae* that occurs in MS Lat 389 is its extended and predominant chains of stepwise motion. Over the course of the *melodiae*, however, ever larger skips (a minor third or greater) become increasingly common. Nevertheless, the relative scarcity of leaps renders them immediately notable to the ear and prompts closer examination of the ways in which they protrude from, or break out of, stepwise motion. The increasing prominence of skips is illustrated in example 8.1A by the fact that the number of notes separating the skipwise motion decreases from thirty-three to one over the course of the *melodiae*—thus indicating ever tighter spacing. (It should be observed, however, that this underlying process is obscured so as to avoid a strict linear progression.)

As the frequency of skips increases, so too do they expand: minor thirds give way to perfect fourths. Additionally, they aggregate into ever extended groups of skips: from two notes (i.e., one interval) to three notes (i.e., two or three grouped intervals) to four notes (three grouped intervals) (see ex. 8.1B, which shows ever extended periods of stepwise motion in M1). These intervals eventually establish their own "chain" in as much as acceleration between them is extinguished in favor of a regularized periodicity (i.e., the exact repetition of the segment marked *x* on ex. 8.1A). What is more, a third statement of *x* is implied immediately after the close of the second with the recurrence of the third (B-flat–G) and eventually the almost obsessive repetition of the major third.

By way of a brief aside, it is also worth noting that by far the most common interval of all the interjecting skips is the minor third (of which there are fourteen statements, as opposed to seven perfect fourths and five major thirds). In addition, it is important to mention that the pitch specific interval of a descending minor third from B-flat to G, occurs seven times throughout the *melodiae*. The significance is evident when one notices that no other interval occurs more than five times (see ex. 8.1C, which shows intervals and interval classes in M1, not in order of appearance).

EXAMPLE 8.1A

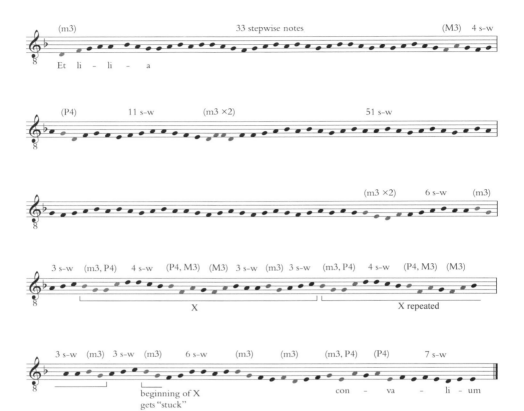

EXAMPLE 8.1B

EXAMPLE 8.1C

The Double Bond of the Reiterated Note

How does one sing a repeated pitch on a long melisma? The question would be redundant if the repeated pitch also marked a change of syllable but, due to the nature of the vocal mechanism, a reiteration of the same pitch on the same vowel cannot be produced without an interruption (however brief) of the sustained vowel. While it is impossible to know for sure how these *melodiae* were sung, there are at least two possible answers to the question posed above. Either the reiterated pitch was sung as such—as two distinct vocalizations—thereby breaking the flow of the melisma, somewhat like a stutter, or the pitch was sustained for twice the length of the standard single note value. Regardless, however, of which solution would have been enforced in performance, the reiterated pitches would have protruded from the texture and thus lingered in the memory of the listener, perhaps even more than the skips. For that reason it is worth taking a closer look at the large-scale contour generated by reiterated pitches, which are highlighted in M1 in example 8.2A.

When all the repeated notes are laid out in the order that they are stated *without* intervening notes (and without repetitions of pairs of repeated notes already stated, as in ex. 8.2B), it is clear that they demarcate an outward spiral from a midpoint (pitch class A), through a tone, major third, perfect fourth, major sixth, and minor seventh to D a perfect fourth above and E a perfect fourth below. It is worth noting that the attempt to break increasingly further away from the initial pitch class A mirrors the process of intervallic expansion described above in the context of the endeavor to break out of stepwise motion.

Of course, example 8.2B is an artificial illustration of what occurs at a *background* level; when one reintroduces the repetitions of reiterated notes (ex. 8.2C shows repeated notes without intervening notes, where the numbers represent the number of notes between pairs), it is evident that the underlying *linear* process of intervallic expansion is obscured by a tendency to "get stuck" on particular reiterated notes (for example, there are two consecutive statements of repeated Bs, two consecutive statements of repeated As, and a further two consecutive statements of repeated Bs toward the end). The tendency to get stuck also occurs in terms of the number of single notes separating each repeated pair. Whereas elsewhere in the *melodiae* the repeated pitches fall into three larger cycles (marked "W," "X," and "Y," respectively, in ex. 8.2C), during each of which they become separated by ever greater groups of notes, thereby giving the impression of a gradual filtering out of repeated notes and a purging of the obstacles to the melismatic flow—the area marked "Z" (also in ex. 8.2C) appears to get stuck, inasmuch as the number of single notes dividing reiterated pitches becomes regularized into a symmetrical pattern of repeated groups of either one or six notes (i.e., 6–1–1–6–6–1–1–6).

The repeated large-scale attempts to purge the *melodiae* of the reiterated-note figure (in the form of cycles, each of which separates the reiterated note figures with ever larger groups of single notes) are complemented by similar processes on a local level. This will be best exemplified by tracing what happens to the initial reiterated figure of the *melodiae* (A–A). First it occurs as a repeated figure, then as two As separated by one note, and eventually as two As separated by three notes and so forth. This process during which statements of pitch class A are spread increasingly further apart repeats by means of various cycles (marked "a," "b," "c," "d," "e," "f," "g," "h," "i" in ex. 8.2D). Thus the means by which the restrictive element (i.e., the repeated A) is overcome in pursuit of "free motion" is at odds with the end. Most of these cycles are separated by areas where the flow seems to get stuck, in as much as the distance between each A is maintained exactly (marked "q," "r," "s," "t," "u" on ex. 8.2D). The background attempt to, as it were, break out of confined space by means of ever greater intervallic distance between initial iterations of repeated notes conflicts with a surface tendency to interrupt flow—of which the repeated note is, in itself, a means.

EXAMPLE 8.2A

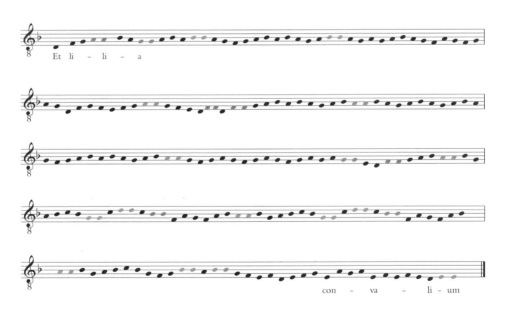

EXAMPLE 8.2B

EXAMPLE 8.2C

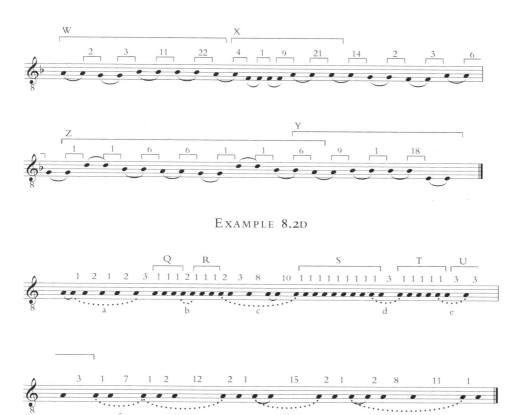

EXAMPLE 8.2D

The Making and Breaking of Chains

Thus "Et lilia" is spun out of the tension between processes of establishing limits (of restricting flow) and processes of overcoming them; in other words the constant battle between the making and breaking of restrictive chains. In this sense the metaphorical application of the term *chains* in this essay is twofold. First, as a linkage mechanism, a chain provides a visual parallel for the long series of notes typical of the Ambrosian *melodiae* (and of Ambrosian chant in general)—where the majority of notes are linked by intervallic "steps" of either a minor or major second. Second, as a bondage tool, *chains* provides a useful analogy for the ways in which musical progression is, at times, inhibited and restricted in the *melodiae*. In this second sense, the "making of chains" refers to the inhibiting of perceived musical motion or development (usually by means of the repetition of particular pitches and motives), while the "breaking of chains" refers to a reinstigation of that sense of motion expanding into new musical areas (by intervallic leaps greater than a second).

The occurrence of *melodiae* at points of particular importance in the Ambrosian liturgy is in keeping with a long tradition, including Cassiodorus and Augustine, that describes melismas as significations of devout ecstasy—liberation from the confines of the mundane and prescribed into the realm of free and divine worship. At a very basic level, the *melodiae* challenge the limits of the human lung capacity. I don't mean to imply that the *melodiae* were intended to be sung as one long breath, but the nature of a melisma is to create the illusion of continuous, flowing breath.

COMPARISON OF *MELODIAE PRIMAE* AND *MELODIAE SECUNDAE*

Immediately noticeable on comparison of these *melodiae primae* (M1) and *secundae* (M2)—notwithstanding the fact that the pitch content of the latter begins a perfect fifth higher than that of the former—is the fact that both start and finish with identical motivic patterns, which might automatically lead to the assumption that they are "versions" of each other. While they are clearly related, however, their sameness ends pretty much as soon as the text does.

If the words "Et lilia convalium" act as a frame for a free internal melisma, then so too do the fixed motifs that accompany them. That is not to say that they do not make use of similar motivic material, because they do (albeit in often varied and ornamented forms). Example 8.3A demonstrates that (despite the misleading exception of the opening of M2), both versions are based on what has been labeled motif *x*.

But the structuring and ordering of the material within each of the *melodiae* differ significantly. The most obvious indications of this are the fact that M2 is thirty-one notes longer than M1 and that M2 spans a major ninth, while M1 has range of an octave. M1 is loosely structured in terms of three progressively longer cycles, during which motif *x*—which occurs at the beginning of each cycle in ever more elaborate guises—is freely elaborated in a complex web of motivic reference dependent on techniques of lengthening, shortening, segmentation, transposition, pitch displacement, and reassemblage, as seen in example 8.3B, where the opening two notes and the final note are common to all three segments. M2, on the other hand, has a far clearer structure: it is built out of six cycles—each of which notably begins with a clear and barely altered statement of the motif before extending and elaborating it—and is framed by what could be heard as an introduction and a coda. This can be seen in example 8.3C. Here, the opening three notes and the final note are common to all segments except the coda, which nonetheless opens with a similar three-note ascent and shares motivic relationships with previous segments as they approach their final Ds (see the bracketed section of the coda). Shaded pitches in this example show notes that were added to a segment that is otherwise similar to the previous one. Arrows indicate identical motives; dotted lines show similar motives between segments.

EXAMPLE 8.3A

EXAMPLE 8.3B

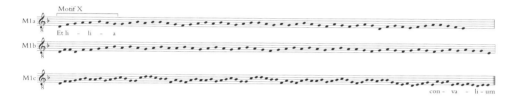

EXAMPLE 8.3C

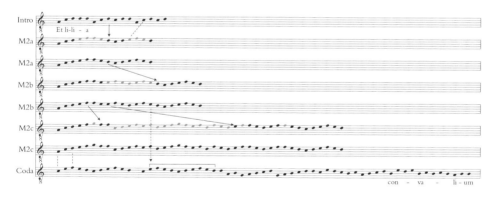

Differences in the treatment of motif *x* are further highlighted when M2 is analyzed in the same way. Example 8.4A shows breaks out of stepwise motion in M2. Example 8.4B shows intervals and interval classes (not in order of appearance) in that *melodiae*. Example 8.4C compares disjunct motion in M1 and M2. Repeated notes in M2 are highlighted in example 8.5A; repeated notes without intervening notes in M2 are shown in example 8.5B, demonstrating a more consistent and exaggerated expansion than in M1. The reduction in example 8.5C clarifies the background contour of emphasized pitches in M2. Example 8.5D compares the treatment of repeated notes in both *melodiae*. Finally, example 8.6 shows the increasing distance between repeated Ds in M2.

Some results differ but demonstrate that similar processes occur in both versions (see the cyclical spreading apart of reiterated notes in example 8.5B and, to a lesser extent, example 8.6, where repeated Ds are spread farther apart from one another but in a somewhat more obsessive, repetitive, and less exaggerated manner than what takes place in M1). Other results, however, show that a complete reversal of M1 processes occurs in M2 (see ex. 8.4A, where skips are initially frequent and become increasingly scarce). At the same time, certain processes that were crucial to M1 are missing in M2—most notably the interval expansion that one would expect in the overall contour generated by the reiterated notes. Instead, most of repeated notes occur on the *same* pitch (F).

EXAMPLE 8.4A

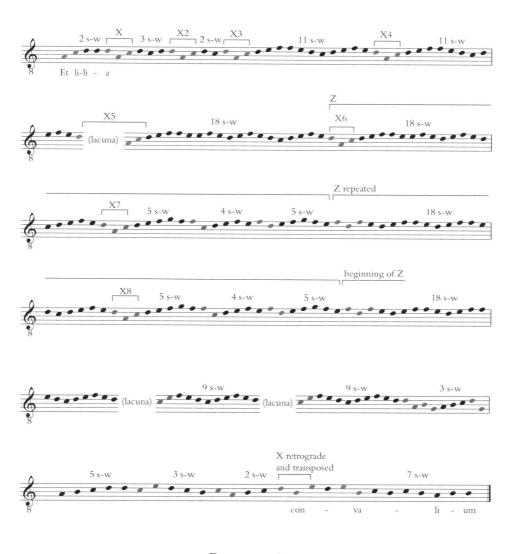

EXAMPLE 8.4B

EXAMPLE 8.4C

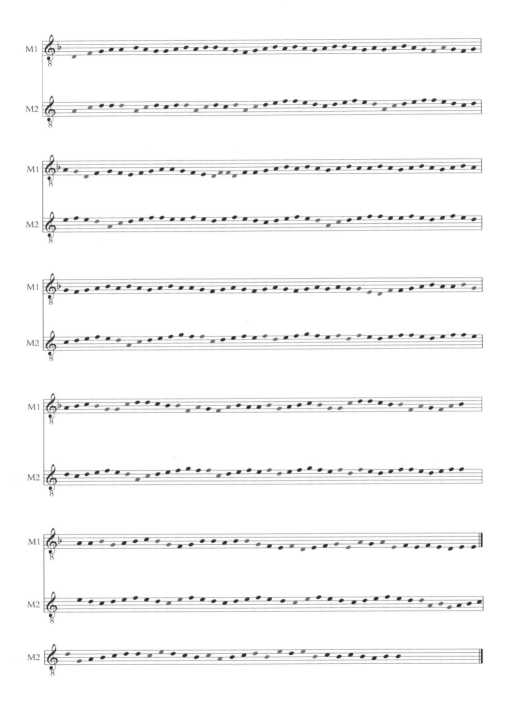

EXAMPLE 8.5A

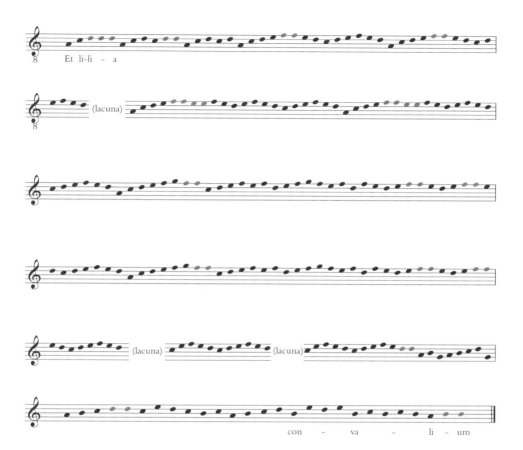

EXAMPLE 8.5B

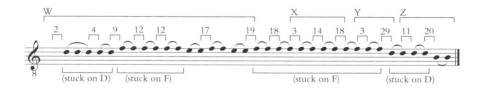

EXAMPLE 8.5C

EXAMPLE 8.5D

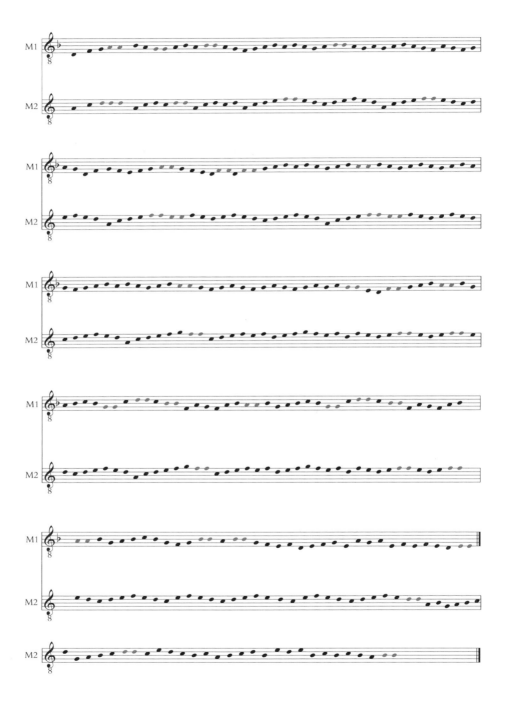

EXAMPLE 8.6

Thus it is clear that even as the processes of free elaboration typical of M1 are exaggerated in M2, so too is the tendency to get stuck. The tension between the breaking and making of chains is exacerbated. In order to assess the extent to which the similarities and differences between M1 and M2 found in this example might illuminate the more general stylistic question posed above—as to the relationship between *melodiae primae* and their *secundae*—it is necessary to evaluate the extent to which these findings might represent consistent patterns. By way of a starting point, a comparison of "Et lilia" with another version found in Lat. liturg. a. 4 might be useful.

Undoubtedly both the Oxford version and the MS Lat 389 version of M1 follow the same model, with the majority of pitches being identical in both manuscripts. There are, however, minor differences that fall into the following categories:

- elaboration/extension of a motive (addition of note/s)
- truncation of a motive (omission of note/s)
- *variation* of a motive (i.e., where the contour and number of notes is the same but pitches have been transposed or pitches have been reordered)
- transposition of motives
- repetition of notes
- insertion of an extra motive
- omission of a motive
- replacement of one motive by another

One common occurrence is the addition or omission of single notes. While these processes cannot neatly or consistently be attributed to one manuscript or the other—as both manuscripts add and omit notes present or absent in the other at various points—the specific points (in terms of the motivic context) at which such processes occur (and thus their "function" within the motivic structure) does appear to be, to some degree, consistent. For example, MS Lat 389 fills in the falling third—a figure that recurs three (perhaps four) times—throughout the *melodiae*. While the addition of notes in MS Lat 389 can in almost all cases be for the purpose of filling in intervals, the addition of notes in Lat. liturg. a. 4 is often for the purpose of reiterating notes.

While there does not appear to be any consistent compression or elaboration of one manuscript in the other—but rather an inconsistent combination of the two—certain differences between the two versions, as subtle and inconsistent as they may appear on a local level, recur in such a way as to suggest that they might be more than simple mistakes on the part of the copyist. But what the logic *is* (if any), be it a gradual stylistic evolution in the *melodiae* over the time period separating the two manuscripts or mere notational error, will remain unclear until further analysis of more versions of "Et lilia" from different time periods as well as of other *melodiae* from different points in the liturgical calendar is undertaken. Only then will it be possible to verify these analytical findings and their relevance to a stylistic definition of the *melodiae*.

Nevertheless, the differences between these two versions of "Et lilia" appear to be largely cosmetic and perhaps most significant are the multiple points of contact, which indicate that the *melodiae* must have been fixed compositions by the time that these manuscripts were compiled. In light of this, it seems likely that the melodic analysis proposed in this paper—which appears to be a useful way of approaching "Et lilia"—might go beyond mere description to have broad application as a tool for the stylistic analysis of this repertoire.

This study has only begun to tip its little toe into what I believe to be a potentially rich sea of exploration. While many of the results provided by this case study have been duplicated in all of the other pairs of *melodiae* I analyzed during the course of my research, any conclusions ventured here can be no more than tentative. A thorough and comprehensive analytical study is necessary to substantiate my findings. The *melodiae* are free and elaborate compositions that resist generalization; nevertheless, investigation of the norms, or lack of norms, underpinning the *melodiae* has been long called for.

Responsory Verse Formulas in the Ambrosian Winter Repertory

John Z. McKay

RESPONSORIES CONSTITUTE THE SECOND-LARGEST DIVISION of the Milanese chant repertory (after the antiphons), but they are the least studied of the major Ambrosian genres. With the exception of a few articles on the *responsoria cum infantibus*, little extensive analysis of responsory melodies has been carried out.[1] David Hiley noted in 1993 the lack of scholarship concerning Ambrosian responsories (and office chants in general):

> Until reliable editions from the early sources and analyses of the
> different genres have been carried out, only general remarks about
> much of the office repertory are possible. . . . Discussion of the
> responsory repertory has concentrated on the elaborate melismas
> in repeat form of the "responsoria cum infantibus" or "cum
> pueris." Much fundamental work remains to be done. It is clear,
> for example, that the various types of responsory ("post hymnum"
> and "ad lectionem" in the morning, "in choro" and "in baptisterio"
> in the evening) use typical melodies and verse formulas, within
> each genre and as a larger group, though less unvaryingly than the
> Gregorian office responsories, and with a number of irregularities
> in the matching of a particular verse tone to a particular final in the
> responsory. But no systematic analyses have been published.[2]

On the whole, Hiley's assessment of the scholarly literature still holds true today, though some of his conclusions require clarification. For example, there appear to be no "typical melodies and verse formulas" specific to *genres* of responsories: all of the formulas discussed below occur in multiple genres. Furthermore, after a rather broad survey, I have found little evidence that liturgical function plays a role in

---

1. For a detailed study of the *responsoria cum infantibus*, see E. T. Moneta Caglio, "I responsori 'cum infantibus' nella liturgia ambrosiana," in Biblioteca Ambrosiana, *Studi in onore di Mons. C. Castiglioni* (Milan: A. Giuffrè, 1957), 481–578. A discussion of the melismas of the *responsoria cum infantibus* in the larger context of Ambrosian chant can be found in Terence Bailey, "Milanese Melodic Tropes," *Journal of the Plainsong and Mediaeval Music Society* 11 (1988): 1–12.

2. David Hiley, *Western Plainchant: A Handbook* (Oxford: Clarendon Press, 1993), 541.

dictating the music of the responsory outside of a general tendency toward certain modes in specific liturgical seasons and the general presence of idiomelic chants on major feast days. On the other hand, there is significant evidence to support Hiley's assertion that particular verse tones are not always associated with a particular final in the responsory. Verse tones do, however, appear to have "home finals" where they are more likely to occur; thus the relationship is not purely random.

Terence Bailey has also noted that some verses "seem like decorated versions of simple tones . . . but others are so elaborate that the rules governing their adaptation to another psalm text are obscure. Many responsory verses have the appearance of free melodies, indistinguishable in style from their responds."[3] The present discussion is a preliminary attempt to clarify and distinguish these simple tones for responsory verses and also to comment on a few tendencies that might produce the "free melodies" that Bailey describes.

The primary source employed for this study was British Library Add. MS 34209 and its edited transcription in volumes 5 and 6 of *Paléographie musicale*.[4] Since this manuscript contains only the winter portion of the Ambrosian liturgical year, any conclusions about general features of Milanese chant must be regarded as tentative. Even this one source, however, provides a large quantity of data for analysis. There are 509 items marked as responsories of some kind, 241 of which have musical notation.[5] These 241 responsories have a total of 257 verses, since a few have multiple verses. Of these 257 verses, about 45 percent follow a set formula, while another 15 percent include a significant portion of a formula but deviate for one or more phrases (see table 9.1). The remaining approximately 40 percent of the responsory verses are therefore idiomelic, a number that seems rather high compared to the frequency of idiomelic verses in the Gregorian and Old Roman repertories.

---

3. Terence Bailey, "Ambrosian Chant," *The New Grove Dictionary of Music and Musicians*, ed. S. Sadie and J. Tyrrell (London: Macmillan, 2001), 1:454.

4. *Paléographie musicale 5–6, Antiphonarium Ambrosianum du Musée Britannique (XIIe siècle), Codex Additional 34209* (1896–1900; repr., Berne: Lang, 1971). Houghton Library MS Lat 388 was also consulted for chants with unusual features; I found no significant variants that would affect the outcome of my responsory verse analyses.

5. Note that this number includes all items marked with "R/" or any version of the word "responsorium," as well as items that are marked as responsories with an editorial note in the transcription. Some confusion exists among some of the scribes in genre designations, so a few of the items marked responsories may in fact be psalmelli. None of the questionable items played a role in the analyses below.

Table 9.1. Formulaic Ambrosian Responsory Verses by Final

Final	Number of notated responsories	Percent of total	Formulaic chants in final	Percent of formulaic chants in final	Variant chants in final	Percent of variant chants in final	Overall formulas and variants
D	75	31.1%	42	56.0%	7	9.3%	65.3%
E	34	14.1%	21	61.8%	3	8.8%	70.6%
F	17	7.1%	9	52.9%	2	11.8%	64.7%
G	97	40.2%	31	32.0%	21	21.6%	53.6%
A	7	3.0%	2	28.6%	2	28.6%	57.1%
B	1	0.4%	0	0.0%	0	0.0%	0.0%
C	10	4.1%	6	60.0%	0	0.0%	60.0%
Total	241	100.0%	111	46.1%	35	14.5%	60.6%

The distribution of finals is quite similar to the statistics compiled by Roy Jesson from over four hundred Ambrosian chants from the mass, demonstrating that this pattern is likely representative of Milanese chant in general. That is to say, there is a marked emphasis on G and D, along with a distribution across other finals that even includes examples on A, B, and C.[6] The combination of final and formula distribution, however, shows a surprising result. While most finals have 50 to 60 percent of verses following a formula, less than a third of chants built on the G final are strictly formulaic. Since G is by far the largest group, composed of over one hundred responsories, the majority of the idiomelic chants occur on the most common final.

The reason for this deviation is unclear, though it should also be noted that there are many significant musical gestures native to the G final. It is possible, given the frequency with which G final responsories occurred, that it was easier to compose new chants out of the familiar segments, resulting in a centonization process that already occurs frequently in the respond sections. Although this is one factor that may have resulted in the great variety of G final verses, another potential explanation will emerge below after the entire family of verse tones has been examined.

Before turning to the Ambrosian verse tones, a few general characteristics of responsory verses should be mentioned. Responsory formulas have already been established for the Gregorian and Old Roman chant repertories.[7] Typical formulas

---

6. See Roy Jesson, "Ambrosian Chant," in Willi Apel, *Gregorian Chant* (Bloomington, Ind.: Indiana University Press, 1958), 480. The only notable difference in Jesson's statistics is the slightly greater percentage of chants with finals on A (a little over double what is seen here), but given the relatively small number of A-mode chants, this difference is probably not significant.

7. For a summary of the Gregorian tones, see *Antiphonale Sarisburiense: A Reproduction in Facsimile*

follow the same general threefold structure as basic psalm tones: an initial melodic gesture (the "intonation," often ascending) set to the first few syllables, a recitation tone, and a closing gesture (or "cadence") set to the last few syllables. Gregorian and Old Roman formulas often have two different phrases following this pattern (i.e., intonation, medial cadence, a new reintonation, and a final cadence); Ambrosian formulas, however, are consistently tripartite in organization—an unusual characteristic for psalm recitation in general.[8] While it is true that the second of the three phrases in Ambrosian formulas is often de-emphasized—particularly when a text is extremely short—there are only a few exceptional cases where it is altogether omitted. Despite these similarities, responsory verse tones also differ significantly from psalm tones: cadences usually stretch over many syllables (often five or more), different reciting tones are sometimes used in the same formula, and the formulas are much more ornate and applied in more complex ways to texts.

Example 9.1 shows a typical family of Ambrosian responsory verses that all follow a similar melodic pattern.[9] The verses are ordered within the example roughly according to families of similar verses, with significant variants of the formula located near the bottom of the example. The labeling system references three characteristic pitches for each verse that often help in classification, namely the final of the responsory and the first and last notes of the verses. The number refers to the page number in the transcription of Add. 34209 in *Paléographie musicale* where the responsory begins. For example, *Egg*-10 represents a responsory with a final on E and a verse that begins on g and ends on g, which can be found on page 10 of the transcription. The most common three-letter sequence for a family of chants will be used to reference the formula: *Egg*-10 is an exemplar of the primary formula for *Egg* verses, so its verse tone will be referred to as the *Egg* formula.

---

of a Manuscript of the Thirteenth Century, ed. Walter Howard Frere (London: Plainsong and Mediaeval Music Society, 1901–24), 4. Tables of both the Gregorian and Old Roman formulas (the latter derived from Vatican City, Biblioteca Apostolica Vaticana, MS San Pietro B79) can be found in Paul Frederick Cutter, "Responsory," *New Grove Dictionary*, 21:224–225. A useful comparison of the two traditions is Joseph Dyer's summary of responsorial psalmody practices. See "Psalm," *Die Musik in Geschichte und Gegenwart*, rev. ed., ed. Ludwig Finscher (Kassel: Bärenreiter, 1994–2007), Sachteil 7:1870.

8. The rare examples of tripartite recitation formulas include the Gregorian and Old Roman invitatory tones and the recitation of the Doxology in the introit. For a summary discussion of both of these genres, see Willi Apel, *Gregorian Chant*, 241–244 and 228–234. A more detailed analysis of the invitatory recitation tones, along with relevant bibliography, can be found in John Caldwell, "The Old Roman Invitatory" in *Cantus Planus, 12th Meeting, Lillafüred/Hungary, 2004*, ed. László Dobszay (Budapest: Hungarian Academy of Sciences, 2006), 231–258. I am grateful to Joseph Dyer for drawing my attention to the importance of the invitatory tones as a useful comparison point for tripartite recitation structures.

9. Neume groupings are not indicated in most of the transcriptions. This was done for clarity, since the layout employed here often produces syllables that stretch across the page. The details of the original notation and neume groupings, however, were considered in sorting and forming correspondences among the verses.

EXAMPLE 9.1A

Egg-10
Vox cla - mán-tis in de - - - - - - sér - to
Egg-90
Jus-ju - rándum quod ju - - - - - - rá - vit
Egg-119
Cae-li e-nárrant gló - - - - - ri - am De - i
Egg-127
Pri-ús - quam mon - tes fi - e - rent
Ebg-27
Tól - li - te por - tas prín - - - - - - ci - pis ves - tri
Egg-243
Qui-a ip-se est tes - - - - - tis et ju - dex
Egg-11
Om-nes gentes pláu - - - - - - di - te má-ni-bus
Egg-128
Ig-ní - tum e-ló-quium tuum ve - he - - - - - - mén - ter
Egg-210
Quaecúm - que vo-vi red - dam ti - bi
Egg-59-I
Ve-ní - te ex-ul-té - - - - - mus in Dómi-no
Egg-59-II
Praeve - ni-á-mus fá-ci-em e-jus in con - fes - si - - - - - - ó - ne
Egg-59-III
Quóni - am De-us mag - - - - nus est Dómi-nus
Dgg-50
Ex Si - on spé-ci-es de - - - - - có - ris e - jus
Egg-176
Quis e - nim in-di - - - - - - cá - vit ti-bi quod nu - dus es - ses
Agg-216
Ho-mo tam - - - - - - - - quam foe-num di - es e - jus
Ggg-264
Dómi - ne ex-áu - di o-ra-ti - ó - nem nos - tram
Acc-37
Spí-ri - tus Sanctus in te in - - - - - - gré-di-tur

EXAMPLE 9.1B

Example 9.1c

Egg-10
rec - tas fá-ci-te sé-mi-tas De - i nos - tri
Egg-90
da - - - - - tú - - - rum se no - bis
Egg-119
an - nún-ti - - - at fir - ma - - - mén - tum
Egg-127
a sáe-cu-lo et in sáe - - - cu - lum
Ebg-27
ut in-tró-e - - at Rex gló - - - ri - - ae
Egg-243
se - cré - - - ta con - sci - - - én - ti - - - a
Egg-11
in vo-ce ex - sul - - - ta - ti - - - - ó - - nis
Egg-128
di - - - - - - - - - lé - xit il - lud
Egg-210
me - - - - - - - - - o Dó - - - mi - no
Egg-59-I
sa - - - - - lu - - - tá - ri nos - - - - - - - tro
Egg-59-II
ju - - - - - bi - - - lé - mus il - - - - - - - li
Egg-59-III
su - - - - - per om - nes de - - - - - - - os
Dgg-50
ma - ni - - - fés - - - te vé - - - ni - - et
Egg-176
ne com - é-de - - - - - res com - e - - - dí - - - sti
Agg-216
i - - - - - - - - - ta flo - - - ré - bit
Ggg-264
ad te per - vé - - - ni - - at
Acc-37
ob - - - - - - um - - - brá - bit ti - - bi

This *Egg* formula begins its first phrase (ex. 9.1A) with an opening intonation of two syllables *g-abcb*, followed by recitation on *b*, and then a cadence of one accent with two preparatory syllables. To see that the cadence is dependent on an accent, we need only note a couple examples of proparoxytones like "mánibus" (*Egg*-11) and "Dómino" (*Egg*-59-I),[10] where the accent falls on the antepenult. These contrast with the prevailing paroxytone ending, as in the first examples of "desérto" (*Egg*-10) and "jurávit" (*Egg*-90), where that accented penultimate syllable receives two pitches, the second of which is sometimes a liquescent (shown here in the verses where the pattern is notated as *bb* instead of *ba*, as in *Egg*-10).

Although this explains the majority of the examples, there are a few other complications to this simple formulaic beginning, since the *Egg* formula is an example of Hiley's reference to responsory verse tones that are not always associated with only one final. As can be seen from the initial letters of the symbols for each example, there are instances of the *Egg* formula in responsories with D, A, and G finals given at the bottom of example 9.1. Moreover, the evidence suggests that there is more than simple borrowing of a formula verbatim into another final. While the D final borrowing is rather straightforward, there are obvious deviations in the borrowings into the A and G finals. The G final borrowing, for example, substitutes a different melody for the normal recitation tone on *b* in the first phrase.

However, the borrowing pattern into the A final is even more idiosyncratic. The inserted gesture in *Agg*-216 has a distinctive contour *adecb*, which is repeated in the second phrase as seen on the next page. Leaps of an ascending fourth are rather rare in E final responsories (both responds and verses), but they appear more frequently in other final chants, such as those with A and C finals. Moreover, although these specific pitches do not occur elsewhere in A final chants, similar contours do appear. Unfortunately, the sample size for A final responsories is quite small (only seven), so it is difficult to draw conclusions about the origin of this figure. Nevertheless, the fact that it occurs twice within *Agg*-216 suggests a deliberate and consistent modification of the typical *Egg* formula. When the figure appears back in the E final in *Egg*-176, it does not occur again in the second phrase. Of course, with only two examples and inconclusive evidence of the melody in the A final, it is difficult to be sure of the direction of borrowing; however, it is clear that borrowing of responsory verse tones into other finals does occur, and it is often accompanied by significant modifications.

One final type of borrowing is apparent in the last example, *Acc*-37. In Gregorian chant, A mode pieces are often transposed versions of another "legitimate" mode, specifically one of the D or E modes. A similar kind of modification is apparent in this responsory verse, which is an *Egg* formula transposed up a fourth. This does not mean, however, that all A final verses in

---

10.　The roman numeral references the first verse out of three verses for the responsory *Egg*-59.

Ambrosian chant are simply transpositions. As will be shown presently, the A and C finals have responsory verses that are formulaic and only appear in those finals. The *Acc*-37 example nonetheless demonstrates that some of the irregular finals in Ambrosian chant *are* transpositions, as in their Gregorian counterparts.[11]

With the exceptions of these irregular finals, the formula is followed remarkably well in the first phrase, although there are some modifications in the borrowed examples and the "Tollite" prefix on *Ebg*-27. Such prefixes are common to variants of responsory verse formulas and appear to be part of a stock repertory of such figures in Ambrosian chant; indeed, sometimes the same prefix occurs in verses constructed on different finals, with the verse otherwise employing gestures and formulas native to its particular final.[12]

The second phrase (ex. 9.1B) contains what appears at first glance to be two different formulas. The first (consistent with the first six chants or so) begins with an intonation of two syllables *g-ab*, is followed by a recitation on *b*, and concludes with a cadence dependent on two accents with one preparatory syllable. The second formula, which is found in many of the verses in the middle of the figure, is little more than a simple melodic turn over four syllables: *b(c)-a-gab-b*, with occasional preparatory syllables on *g*. The *Egg*-11 verse appears to be a hybrid of the two. However, on closer inspection, the formula is simply dependent on the number of syllables available. If there are only four syllables, the second formula is used. If there are five or six, an intermediate form is employed, and only if there are seven or more syllables (and the accents fall at the right place) is the longer first formula used.

Formulaic rules with this level of complexity suggest that the principles must have been systematized somehow; perhaps they were known as a "long formula" and a "short formula" for this phrase. The only other explanation would have to assume either that all the chants in this formula were composed together or that old examples within the formula were consulted when a new chant was composed. If these chants were created at different times while transmission was still primarily oral, the composers of new verses in this formula must have been aware of not only basic treatment of syllables and accents but also specific variants to be used when the text was of unusual length.

---

11.   This chant is sung on the Saturday before the last Sunday of Advent (i.e., the feast of the Annunciation in the Ambrosian liturgical calendar), a liturgical day with a number of other irregularities in musical structure. Perhaps the most significant deviation is another responsory verse, *Egd*-35 (*Myrrha gutta et cassia*), which begins on the wrong note and has two different recitation tones on *g* and *e*. As mentioned above, different recitation pitches occur in Gregorian responsory verses but are not found in any of the Ambrosian formulas. Given the unique features of these two chants, perhaps further investigation into the chants for this day is warranted to determine whether the music has other unusual borrowings and misuses of formulas that might indicate whether they have been composed together, perhaps at a later date.

12.   An example of this pattern is the verse *Gad*-5 (*Deus virtutum*), which uses the same prefix as *Egd*-35 (*Myrrha gutta et cassia*) and *Ead*-111/*Ead*-126 (*Magi venerunt*).

Turning to example 9.1C, the final phrase consists of an intonation of one syllable *gab*, a recitation on *b*, and an elaborate cursive cadence of five syllables.[13] The variation of the extra syllable in *Egg*-243 (on "conscientia") does not have a clear explanation, but the unusual treatment of the last two syllables in *Egg*-119 ("firmamentum") and *Egg*-128 ("dilexit illud") may have something to do with the closed consonants on the penultimate syllable.[14] If there are not enough syllables for this formula, then abbreviated versions (such as those in *Egg*-128 and *Egg*-210) are used. Immediately below these, the *Egg*-59 verses that are braced together (all from the same responsory) contain an additional suffix, which is unique to that responsory.[15]

One final question about the *Egg* formula concerns the treatment of some of the short texts. As noted above, the second and third phrases have alternate versions if there are not enough syllables, but some of the examples have used up most of the text in the first phrase, so they do not have enough text to fill out the formulas for the remainder (e.g., *Egg*-128). The simplest explanation is that the formulas are applied so that phrase breaks occur at syntactically appropriate places in the text. Almost all of the second phrases begin either with a conjunction ("et," "aut," "nisi"), a preposition ("ad"), or a relative pronoun ("quem"). Where possible, the rest begin new sentences. These patterns constitute clear evidence that formulas are applied to texts with sensitivity not only to accents and syllable counts but also to grammatical structures, even when the tripartite formula organization makes this difficult.

While the *Egg* formula and its variants demonstrate many of the characteristic features of Ambrosian responsory verses, there are further questions raised by other formulas. One such example can be seen in example 9.2, which shows the first phrase of the *Ffa* formula, the only formula for the F final. Here, instead of the use of a recitation tone for extra text, the pattern provides almost every syllable with its own pitch, using reintonations where necessary. Given the great variety of possible text lengths, it is difficult to create abstract rules to generalize all the details

---

13. Note that the consistent appearance of a third intonation confirms the tripartite verse structure discussed above.

14. Obviously, the distinction between a nasal consonant ("firmame*n*tum") and a liquid ("il*l*ud") weakens the comparison between the variants, though no other explanation is immediately apparent. In general, liquescents appear to play a small role in variants of some formulas, but given the relative infrequency of liquescents occurring at pivotal points within a phrase, it is difficult to draw specific conclusions.

15. This is a fairly common feature of responsories with multiple verses. They generally follow a consistent formula for all the verses of a given responsory, and about half of the time, the verse formula is based on a standard formula, often with a bit of elaboration as in the *Egg*-59 verses here. Multiple verse responsories with their own unique formula are also common, however, particularly on major feast days. An example of this pattern can be seen in the six *Ede*-294 and *Edf*-294 verses for Good Friday accompanying the responsory *Foderunt manus meas*.

EXAMPLE 9.2

into a coherent formula.[16] Moreover, the boundary between chants that follow the *Ffa* formula and those that simply borrow some material (such as an intonation

---

16. The tendency to set every syllable to its own pitch in the *Ffa* formula also results in unusual variations in the middle of verses. In addition to a standard second and third phrase, chants in this formula often introduce a fourth phrase inserted between the first and second phrases that is generally a combination of formulaic elements derived from a combination of the first two phrases of the formula (e.g., *Ffa*-148, *Fca*-125, *Fcc*-174, *Gff*-256).

or cadence pattern) becomes ever more difficult to draw.[17] Some gestures, such as the *f-a-c* intonation from this formula, become so common that many verses and responds, both in the F final and in other finals, make use of them before diverging into an otherwise idiomelic chant.[18]

Another issue arises concerning the status of groups of only two or three chants that share a common formula. Two such groups are shown in examples 9.3 and 9.4, the *Acb* responsory verses and the *Ddf* variants.[19] The *Acb* responsories are only found in the *A* final, but there is clearly a possibility that they are modeled on each other, given their liturgical proximity (in feria II and feria III during the first week of Lent). This case is thus similar to the case of multiple verses for one responsory, where the formula may or may not be related to a standard one, but verses in close proximity on the same final are set to the same basic blueprint.

EXAMPLE 9.3

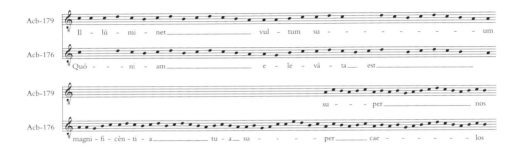

---

17. Some of the examples of chants that lie slightly outside the boundaries of the verses shown in
     example 9.3 include *Fcd*-163 (*Deus ne elonges a me*), which transposes some of the cadences and
     the gestures of the *Ffa* formula down a fifth. Even outside of the *F* final, verses like *Gff*-257
     (*Angelus qui eruit me*) and *Gfg*-204 (*Quoniam iniquitates meae*) incorporate significant segments of
     the *Ffa* formula, but otherwise use gestures more common to the G final.

18. The variation in the first phrases of *Fca*-125 and *Fcc*-174 here may well be another example of
     such a stock pattern, which has similarities to some responds. The latter portions of the verses
     Ffa-81 and *Dfa*-12 also contain long inserted melismas that are almost identical.

19. Many other such families exist, including well-defined examples such as the *Edf* chants—*Edf*-
     181 (*Averte faciem tuam*) and *Edf*-187 (*Domine Deus salutis meae*)—and less clearly defined families,
     such as numerous variants of the *Ggg* and *Ggb* formulas.

EXAMPLE 9.4

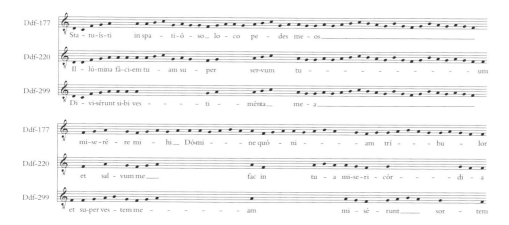

The *Ddf* variant situation is quite different. The verses all begin with an intonation similar to a standard *Ddf* formula modeled in a couple dozen chants. However, an extended melisma is introduced that is not in the original formula, and the rest of the verses contain further minor deviations.[20] This melisma is consistent across wide gaps in the manuscript, suggesting, again, that it might be one of a set of stock phrases of Ambrosian chant.

A final problem is posed by the verses of the *Ccd* formula, shown in example 9.5. The majority of chants with a final on C use segments of common formulas, but the broad group of chants shown here have little in common between the opening intonation and the penultimate cadence. Yet there are clearly a number of melodic fragments and contours that are shared among various verses in this group.[21] Although the formula correspondence is not perfect, there is much more consistency in the penultimate cadence and the final phrase than would be expected if a formula were not used, even if it is preceded by various small segments of C–mode chant seemingly freely combined.

---

20.   A summary of the primary *Ddf* formula (without melisma) can be seen in example 9.6.

21.   One of the melodic fragments, found most clearly on "peccata nostra" in *Ccd*-306, involves a contour beginning on an ascending perfect fourth *dga-f-ef-efededc*, which is a transposition up a fourth of the melody discussed above in the *Egg* formula exemplified by verses *Egg*-176 and *Agg*-216. This melodic gesture appears to be a common feature to both A- and C-final chants.

EXAMPLE 9.5

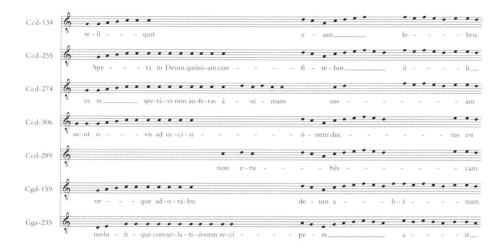

Considering the standards of the traditional eight-mode system of Gregorian practice, it may seem remarkable that Ambrosian chant has a responsory tone based on a C final, though this formula appears almost exclusively at that pitch level. The only deviation is a transposition to G in *Gga-235*, although this is probably an aberration rather than the standard final for this formula. The unusual character of responsories employing this final is further emphasized by their distinctive melodic character and the fact that they are sung on specific liturgical days: all the examples of C final responsories occur in the week after Christmas and the week before Easter.[22]

The relatively unstable nature of the introductory and middle phrases of the *Ccd* formula is also reminiscent of G-final verses. As mentioned above, even though the largest group of Ambrosian responsories have a final on G, relatively few of them follow a recognizable formula exactly. The G-final verses use different melodic segments of chant than those found in the *Ccd* formula, but the process of combination is similarly uncertain. However, it is clear that there are two G-final formula archetypes, *Ggg* and *Ggb*. At this point, it will be helpful to refer to example 9.6, which contains a summary of all eight verse formulas in the Ambrosian responsory repertory.[23] Each of these has at least six clear exemplars (the *Ccd* formula is the smallest), but most have a dozen or more.

22. Other finals also seem to be associated loosely with liturgical seasons. For example, all but one of the A final responsories occur during Lent, but no F-mode responsories are used during Lent.

23. Michel Huglo has mentioned (personal correspondence, October 2007) an unpublished study done in the 1950s by Raffaele Baratta at the Pontificio Istituto di Musica Sacra that found similar verse formulas in Milanese responsories. Moreover, Baratta was apparently working from tables prepared by Dom Gregory Suñol at the Pontificio Istituto di Musica Sacra. I have not had access to these materials in preparing this article.

EXAMPLE 9.6

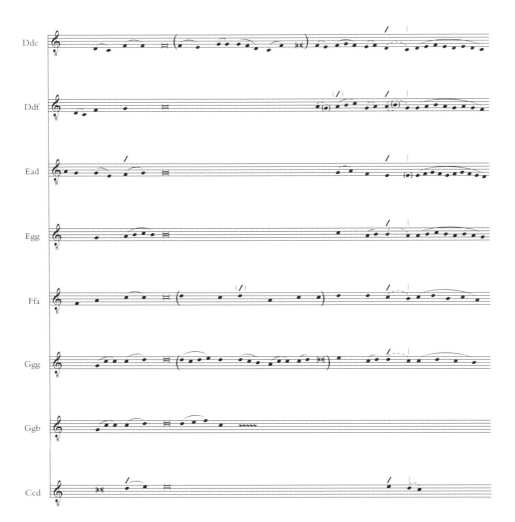

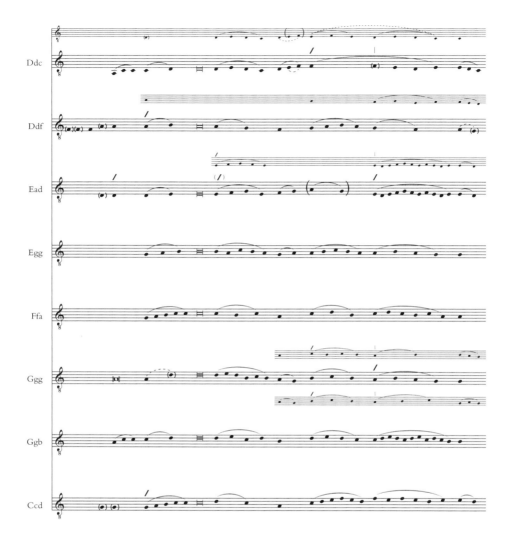

Looking at the G-final tones, the most immediately apparent feature is that they share a common initial intonation. Although a "purer" form of these two formulas is given, the situation is much more complex than what is shown in the example. Of the chants that match these two formulas, about a third are clearly *Ggg*, a third are clearly *Ggb*, and a third are somewhere in the middle. That is to say, the end of the first phrase and the entire second phrase often contain musical gestures that are a mixture of the two formulas and sometimes miscellaneous G-final gestures. The only reliable way to differentiate them is, as with the *Ccd* formula, to look at the final phrase. The final phrases of the G-final verses clearly divide into two groups as represented in example 9.6, with the *Ggg* formula accommodating a few proparoxytone variants.

This similarity between the two G-final formulas may provide another explanation for the large percentage of idiomelic verses on the G final. Obviously, given the number of intermediate cases, these two formulas are not quite stable, and perhaps this instability led to a general feeling that G-final responsories were well suited to freely composed verses, given the uncertainty around actual formulas.

It seems convenient that we have ended up with exactly eight verse tones, just as in Old Roman and Gregorian chant. Although this pattern may be suggestive, it is probably coincidental, and no conclusions about possible connections to the eight-mode system should be drawn (particularly given that there is only one F-final formula and there is a clear group of verses with a final on C). However, the ambitus of each Ambrosian verse tone spans a segment of the overall gamut, and collectively these formulas cover the scale from bottom to top in a similar way to the modal verse organization of other repertories. While obviously drawing on different principles than the eight-mode system, the responsory verse tones give clear evidence that some Milanese chants are founded on formulas that relate to a particular final, a conclusion that suggests that some previous scholarship downplaying the possibilities of Ambrosian "modality" should be reconsidered. On the question of the number of and distribution of tones and their relationship to finals, it should also be noted that previous scholars, including Walter Frere and Helmut Hucke, have discussed possible responsory tones beyond the traditional eight in Gregorian chant (even in the old core repertory).[24] There is still much to be determined in all chant repertories about the relationship of responsory verse formulas to early organizations of modal systems.

Is it possible that there were older tones, even perhaps based on other finals, and that through them we could make a connection between regional repertories that might hint at more ancient similarities? Any answer at this point is purely speculative. However, some final suggestive elements of this comparison become apparent when all the various verse formulas are lined up as in example 9.6. A few features of the cadences of the final phrase are most noteworthy. First, the final cadences do not depend on accent; a few places where accents often occur are marked, but these aspects of the formulas are inconsistently applied. Second, and more strikingly, all of the primary cadential forms follow five-syllable patterns. These pentasyllabic cursive cadences call to mind Frere's conclusion that cadences in Gregorian responsory verses were dependent on five syllables, regardless of

---

24. See the discussion in Hiley, *Western Plainchant*, 65–66. Further details can be found in Frere's introduction and in David Hiley's revised version of Hucke's *MGG* article. See David Hiley and Helmut Hucke, "Responsorium," *Die Musik in Geschichte und Gegenwart*, Sachteil 8:176–200.

accent.[25] Indeed, even medieval discussions of responsorial singing make reference to some of these features, including Aurelian's remark in chapter 19 of his *Musica disciplina*: "We pray the singer to begin concluding all the verses of the nocturnal responses from the fifth syllable before the end; and this is according to the musicians who have maintained that not more than five waves of the sea also remove all storms from the same."[26] Although any conclusions about the potential modal connections between Milanese chant and other repertories must remain tentative, the cadential structure of the Ambrosian responsory verses suggests an ancient link to the same source as Gregorian responsorial practices. Future studies on Ambrosian responsories will undoubtedly shed more light on the possible connections across chant repertories and offer further clues to the ancient musical practices from which they were derived.

I would like to thank Thomas Forrest Kelly for all of his insights and suggestions concerning the research that resulted in this article; his encouragement and mentorship have been invaluable at every stage of the project.

---

25. A more recent evaluation of this aspect of Frere's work, as well as a comprehensive review of problems of accent in cadential structures in Gregorian chant, can be found in Terence Bailey, "Accentual and Cursive Cadences in Gregorian Psalmody," *Journal of the American Musicological Society* 29, no. 3 (Autumn 1976): 463–471.

26. Aurelian of Reome, *The Discipline of Music (Musica disciplina)*, trans. Joseph Ponte (Colorado Springs: Colorado College Music Press, 1968), 50. "Id autem oramus cantorem ut omnium versuum fines in nocturnalibus responsoriis a quinta incipiat desinere syllaba ante finem ultime. Et hoc secundum musicos qui non amplius quam quinque assevere maris undas, et ex eisdem omnes eximeri procellas." The edited Latin version is from *Aureliani Reomensis Musica disciplina*, ed. Lawrence Gushee, Corpus Scriptorum de Musica 21 (Rome: American Institute of Musicology, 1975), 124. I am indebted to Barbara Haggh-Huglo for bringing this reference to my attention.

Ambrosiana at Harvard:
New Sources of Milanese Chant
is the third volume of the
HOUGHTON LIBRARY STUDIES
and was
designed and typeset
in Bembo by Duncan G. Todd
and printed by Universal Millennium, Inc.